The Transformation of Georgia from 2004 to 2012

Dimitri Gvindadze

The Transformation of Georgia from 2004 to 2012

State Building, Reforms, Growth and Investments

Second Edition

palgrave
macmillan

Dimitri Gvindadze
London, UK

The book reflects personal views of Author and not those of any of the author's employers

ISBN 978-3-031-18263-1 ISBN 978-3-031-18264-8 (eBook)
https://doi.org/10.1007/978-3-031-18264-8

This Palgrave Macmillan imprint is published by the registered company Springer Nature Switzerland AG
The registered company address is: Gewerbestrasse 11, 6330 Cham, Switzerland

To Ukraine's fight for freedom

Contents

List of Figures

List of Tables

CHAPTER 1

Reforms, State Building and the Legacy

Abstract This chapter shows what Georgia achieved in 2004–2012 in terms of growth, investment and fight against corruption. It reviews the rest of the book which explains how Georgia achieved this, which pitfalls to avoid and how to think of a state building. Key messages: (1) economic convergence with high-income countries can only happen through a comprehensive state-building process in which multiple internal and external factors amplify each other; (2) economics alone is an insufficient guide to development; and (3) unique paths of the economic convergence must be implemented by national leaders and they cannot be outsourced.

Keywords Growth · Reforms · Investment · Corruption · State Building

Born in the 1970s, my generation is the last to remember the Soviet twilight, the Soviet break-up in 1991 and the transition from communism to capitalism. Three decades after the end of the Soviet Union were enough for fully post-Soviet generations to mature. And yet, at the start of the third decade of the twenty-first century, the post-Soviet space is often called the "early transition region."

How many years would it take a lower-middle-income country at a gross domestic product (GDP) per capita of US$ 4,000 (Georgia's GDP

D. Gvindadze, *The Transformation of Georgia from 2004 to 2012*,
https://doi.org/10.1007/978-3-031-18264-8_1

per capita in 2012—the end of the period discussed in this book—was US$ 4410) to catch up with, say, Croatia, Hungary or Poland where GDP per capita in 2019 was estimated by the International Monetary Fund at approximately US$ 15,000–17,000?[1] Around 15 years, if annual nominal growth of GDP per capita in US$ terms is 10%. Sustained growth at this level means (1) benign external economic environment and mitigation of geopolitical risks; (2) no major growth reversals or exchange rate adjustments, hence no accumulation of external and internal economic imbalances; (3) high growth of a volume of output which in the context of a stagnant demographics implies continuous improvement in productivity; and (4) stable inflation expectations. Even in this benign scenario, the convergence takes more than 15 years because Croatia, Hungary and Poland continue growing in real terms, they have a more stable geopolitics (NATO and the European Union membership) and they have more stable exchange rates, which brings my generation—people in their late forties at the time of writing of this book—to the retirement age. A whole "life in transition," with instability, insecurity and anxiety.

Hence key questions in this book:

- What is the nexus between economic policies and geopolitical, political, emotional, historical, social and cultural norms, forces and factors which shape the process of the national development? Can a scholar or a policymaker deliver a right diagnosis and prescribe a right treatment without comprehending and acting on the critical mass of these interconnections?
- Do low- to middle-income countries reform to add one or two percentage points to their growth rates, winning themselves international accolades for their "growth exceeding expectations," or do they do it to join—in a lifetime—the club of advanced nations? Is the goal of public leaders to orchestrate leaps "from third world to first" tolerating no halfways, or to be content with a mediocre positive outcomes?
- What can strengthen the "winds of change" in the "early transition region" where domestic barricades against such change exist and when the world order is creating headwinds?

[1] International Monetary Fund. World Economic Outlook database (January 2020).

This book focuses on Georgia in 2004–2012—the nine years between the "Revolution of Roses" in Tbilisi in November of 2003 which brought to power a reformist pro-Western political force and the parliamentary elections in October of 2012 in which it was defeated. The book explains what can be accomplished in two electoral terms at a given starting level of GDP per capita and which pitfalls to avoid. It contributes to documenting a decade-long history of Georgia.

The book explains how Georgia—a small resource-poor economy in the complex region—sustained high growth, reduced crime and corruption, anchored itself to radars of investors and modernized infrastructure and institutions. It explains how Georgia's transformation in 2004–2012 attempted to reach the "escape velocity." In physics, the escape velocity is the speed to which an object needs to accelerate to escape a gravitational pull of a massive body. Unless such velocity is reached, an object falls back to the massive body. The stronger this gravitational pull, the higher the escape velocity must be. Same in the national development. The weaker the starting position (Georgia's starting position in 2004 was weak, as explained in this book), the more determined and comprehensive the state building must be to escape the gravitational pull of the past. Note the difference between individual reforms and the state building. Whereas the term "state building" has an unequivocally positive directional connotation, the word "reform" is directionally more nebulous. State building may create lasting legacies. Isolated reforms cannot.

This book explains main variables in Georgia's state-building equation of 2004–2012 and how Georgia tried to solve that equation. It builds on—and stretches far beyond—the first edition of this book published in 2017 which devoted less space to emotional, historical, societal, geopolitical and political enablers of the national development.[2] This book's chapters on Georgia's geopolitics, on public leadership, national governance, market-based sectoral policies, territorial development and urbanization, dollarization and elections in 2012 are new. Other chapters are expanded and updated.

I show how Georgia was looked at—and how Georgia's leaders in 2004–2012 wanted it to be looked at—by a global investor on its quest for a destination. Georgia centered as it is, the book can help state builders and reformers elsewhere, although conceptualization, sequencing and

[2] D. Gvindadze (2017).

scoping of the state building cannot be replicated indiscriminately. The book can help public leaders to deliver on political changes they trigger, to manage expectations and to communicate with voters, including the statistically significant "I-will-vote-for-whoever-lowers-my-retirement-age" voters.

The book contributes to a discussion on the "economic convergence" where economists mainly write on economics, political scientists and international relations professionals on politics and diplomacy, though bringing *all* these insights together is often a challenge. Economics alone is the insufficient guide to development. A growth regression is pointless without many explanatory variables which influence each other. Accurate solutions to such regressions do not exist. Economic theories are often incremental and insufficiently maximalist. Yet, maximalism is what low-to middle-income countries need to orchestrate breakthroughs. Paths of rapid convergence with advanced nations are replete with risks and idiosyncrasies stretching beyond the realm of the economics.

Many bestsellers on development take broad cross-country views, though development can only be national. Its multiple elements cannot be captured by scholars focusing on many countries at once, irrespective of their academic credentials. When you zoom out—write about a country on the basis of a desk research without living in it sufficiently long—you end up in a stylized ecosphere in which simple unidirectional causalities prevail over chaotic correlations and uncertainties which define our lives. Authors of books on the economic development are vulnerable to what Nassim Nicholas Taleb calls: (1) the *illusion of understanding* in which the world is more complicated and random than many realize (the *narrative fallacy*—when humans overinterpret and sterilize stories to make them compact and coherent and enhance their memorizability—increases our *impression* of understanding at the expense of the raw truth) and (2) the *retrospective distortion* in which description of events *as they unfold* without knowledge of their final outcomes differs from an *ex post description of* the same events which gets corrupted by knowledge of the outcomes of these events. Point (2) is related to our predisposition to a *confirmation bias* in which, for example, researchers seek to corroborate their original hypotheses.[3] The way to mitigate these illusions, fallacies, distortions and biases is to have a real-time insider familiarity with the

[3] N. Taleb (2010).

subject (so that the retrospective assessment is balanced out with experience of events as they unfold) and to focus on as many elements of the national development equation as possible.

For most of the period explained in this book, I worked in the government of Georgia (I have never been a member of any political party) and watched events from the inside as they unfolded. This hopefully mitigates risks of the "confirmation bias" and of the "retrospective distortion." I also think that "watching events as they unfold" is useful but insufficient for an informed view on events. A retrospective judgment enriches the understanding of successes and failures. Hence, my procrastination with this second edition of the book, which enhanced my memories of 2004–2012 with a retrospective thinking, crystallized with the passage of time. To mitigate the narrative fallacy risk, I tried to elaborate on multiple factors influencing Georgia's development in 2004–2012.

I seek to bridge the gap between technical reports prepared, for example, by international financial institutions and other publications on Georgia's transformation in 2004–2012 which (1) are almost entirely qualitative, (2) do not offer the same cross-country perspective and (3) do not focus on the same set of factors as in this book.

Nine years explained in this book are eternity for politicians and citizens. But in historic terms they are a blink of an eye. Lasting legacies are created through decades of an uninterrupted state building. This book must be read having this in mind. Any success—unless there is a lasting regional peace and stability in the Caucasus and in global geopolitics on which such regional peace depends—is subject to bumpy rides and reversals. Predictive quality of the past is weak. A state building may or may not trigger a lasting legacy. The first three decades of Georgia's post-Soviet transition were so complex that they cannot be extrapolated into the future without blunders.

This book is not a deep dive into all circumstances and factors which influenced Georgia in 2004–2012 (domestic politics, geopolitics, national security, law enforcement, administration of justice, etc.), or into multiple sectoral reforms implemented in 2004–2012. Such reforms can be best discussed by people who drove them. In this sense, I seek to convey the spirit of the state building, to elaborate, within the historical and political context, on a cross-sectoral mainstay of Georgia's transformation and global economic positioning in 2004–2012. Because of my background, I devote more space to economics and finance.

In this first chapter, I show *what* Georgia achieved in 2004–2012: one of the highest per capita growth rates in Europe (Table 1.1, Figs. 1.1, 1.2 and 1.3), one of the highest volumes of inbound foreign direct investment (FDI) in Europe (Figs. 1.4 and 1.5) and one of the best advances in the fight against corruption globally (Fig. 1.6). In subsequent chapters, I explain *how* Georgia achieved this and which pitfalls to avoid.

According to the Transparency International's Global Corruption Barometer 2010–2011 (the latest report in the period 2004–2012), Georgia had the highest percentage of people, *globally*, who believed that corruption decreased.[4] Perception of corruption in public institutions in Georgia was the fifth lowest *globally*, after Denmark, Switzerland, Finland and Norway. Percentage of Georgians who reported paying bribe to public institutions (around 3.5%) was one of the lowest *globally*, putting Georgia into the same league with Denmark, Norway, UK, Switzerland, Finland, Germany, Australia, South Korea, Netherlands, Iceland and Portugal. Some 77% of respondents in Georgia thought that their government was "effective or very effective" in its fight against corruption—the second highest percentage *globally*.

According to the Worldwide Governance Indicators (Fig. 1.6), in 2004–2012 Georgia had the third best improvement—*globally*—in the "control of corruption" estimate and the second-best improvement—*globally*—in the "rule of law" estimate.

Chapters 2 and 3 discuss last years of the Soviet Union and Georgia's early post-Soviet transition up to the Revolution of Roses in 2003. What brought down the Soviet Union? Why did the Perestroika trigger an avalanche of events escaping anyone's imagination? What did the Soviet Union leave in its wake in Georgia? What was Georgia before the Revolution of Roses and what caused the revolution? How did all those years influence emotional, social, economic, political and geopolitical features of Georgia? The chapters recount my personal memories and they do not represent a piece of historical scholarship.

Chapter 4 examines the depth of Georgia's economic downfall immediately after the Soviet break-up. Which constraints did this impose on leaders of the Revolution of Roses? Could a growth breakthrough happen through a piecemeal path-dependent change? Why did a mismatch

[4] Percentage of Georgians that thought corruption increased stayed the same or decreased in the past three years: 78% decreased; 13% stayed the same; 9% increased (TI Global Corruption Barometer dataset).

Table 1.1 Georgia in 2003–2012

	2003	*2012*	*CAGR**
Georgia's rank in the World Bank's Doing Business indicators (global rank, 185 countries)	137th (2004)	9th (2013)	
Georgia's rank in the Heritage Foundation Index of Economic Freedom (global rank, 177 countries)	78th (2004)	21st (2013)	
Georgia's sovereign credit ratings (Standard and Poor's/Fitch/Moody's)	–	BB-/BB-/Ba3	
Gross Domestic Product, current prices (US$ billion)**	4.1	16.5	16.7%
Gross Domestic Product, current prices (GEL billion)**	8.8	27.2	13.4%
Gross Domestic Product, constant prices (GEL billion)**	17.8	30.4	6.1%
Gross Domestic Product, current prices, purchasing power parity (international dollar, billion)***	16.4	36.6	9.3%
Gross Domestic Product per capita, current prices (US$)	1,034	4,410	17.5%
Gross Domestic Product per capita, current prices, purchasing power parity (international dollar)	4,145	9,799	10.0%
Openness of the economy (sum of exports and imports of goods and services in percent of GDP)	79%	96%	
Government Effectiveness (World Bank composite index range from –2.5 to 2.5: higher values mean government institutions more mature and responsive)	−0.5	0.6	
General government revenue in percent of GDP	15.5%	27.7%	
General government total expenditures in percent of GDP	16.1%	28.4%	
General government gross debt in percent of GDP	61.4%	33.5%	
Current account balance in percent of GDP	−9.4%	−11.4%	
General government debt in percent of gross external debt	53%	32%	
Monetary authorities' debt in percent of gross external debt	12%	4.3%	

(continued)

Table 1.1 (continued)

	2003	*2012*	*CAGR**
Gross external debt in percent of GDP	72%	84%	
Official reserve assets of the central bank (US$ billion)	0.2	2.87	34.4%
Total assets of commercial banks (GEL billion)	1.34	14.35	30.1%
Total assets of commercial banks in percentage of GDP (end of period)	16%	55%	
USS/GEL exchange rate (GEL per US$, end of period)	2.075	1.6567	

Sources Geostat, National Bank of Georgia, The World Bank (open data), International Monetary Fund. World Economic Outlook Database (October 2020)

*CAGR means 'compound annual growth rate'. CAGR 2004-2012 is calculated using the formula: ((value in 2012/value in 2003)^(1/9))−1. In other words, in this table CAGR is annual rate of growth which allows a value in 2003 to grow to value in 2012

**GDP at current prices means nominal GDP; GDP at constant prices means real GDP. Change in real GDP thus measures change in volume of output without factoring in a change in prices. Change in nominal GDP measures change in both volume of output and of price level measured by GDP deflator. Nominal GDP real GDP and GDP deflator are linked by the formula: nominal GDP = real GDP*(GDP deflator/100). In terms of rate of change, (1+rate of change in nominal GDP)=(1+rate of change in real GDP)*(1+rate of inflation measured by the GDP deflator)

***Purchasing power parity (PPP) is the rate at which currency in one country needs to be converted into currency of another country for it to buy the same amount of goods in both countries. GDP at PPP is thus GDP converted to international dollars applying PPP conversion rate. PPP conversion is used because, for example, a fixed amount of US$ can buy more in a country with lower prices than in a country with high prices, so a buyer's purchasing power in the two countries is different despite possession of the same nominal amount of US$

between a stock and a flow of wealth which emerged by the middle of the 1990s lead to a significant social disruption and anxiety which complicated a rapid transformation? What are general takeaways on growth and modernization of developing countries and societies?

Chapter 5 explains the link between national security and state building. The link is important because sovereignty and territorial integrity are preconditions for development. How does Russia's geopolitical revisionism influence Georgia's security and national governance? To what extent are liberal democracies and open societies protected against geopolitical actors which exploit such liberalism and openness?

Chapter 6 discusses three key qualities of a successful public leadership: vision, courage and altruism. A leader devoid of even one of these three

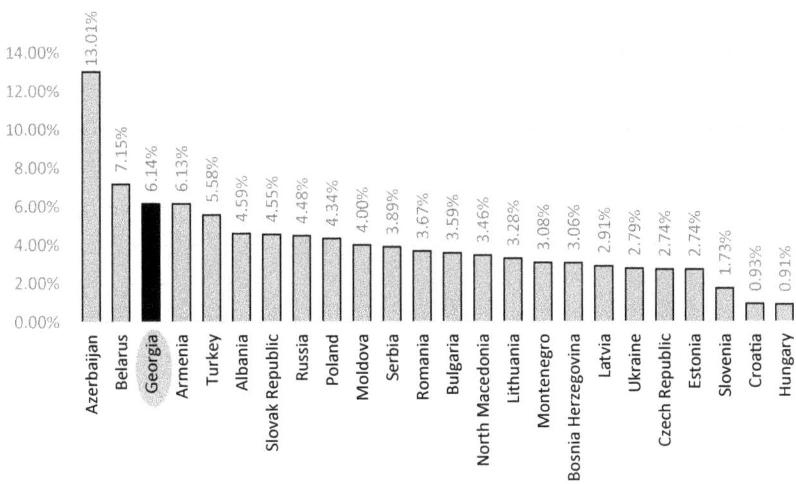

Fig. 1.1 CAGR, real GDP growth in 2004–2012 (constant prices, national currency) (*Source* International Monetary Fund. World Economic Outlook databse [October 2020])

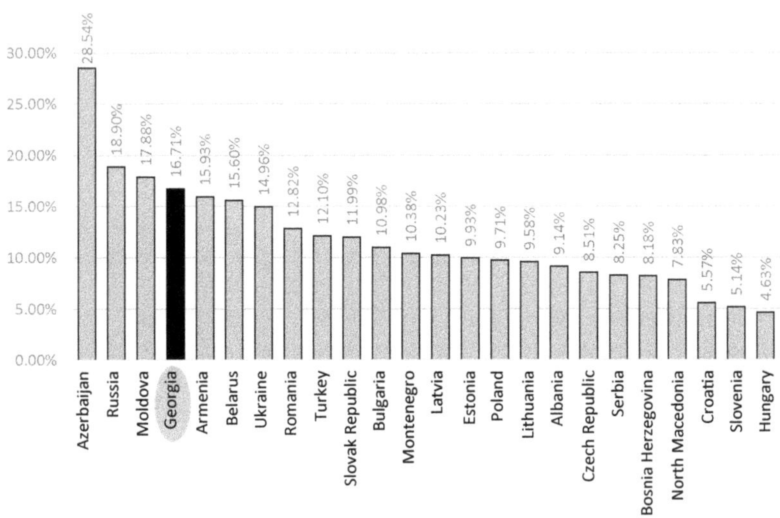

Fig. 1.2 CAGR, GDP growth in 2004–2012 (US$, current prices) (*Source* International Monetary Fund. World Economic Outlook databse [October 2020])

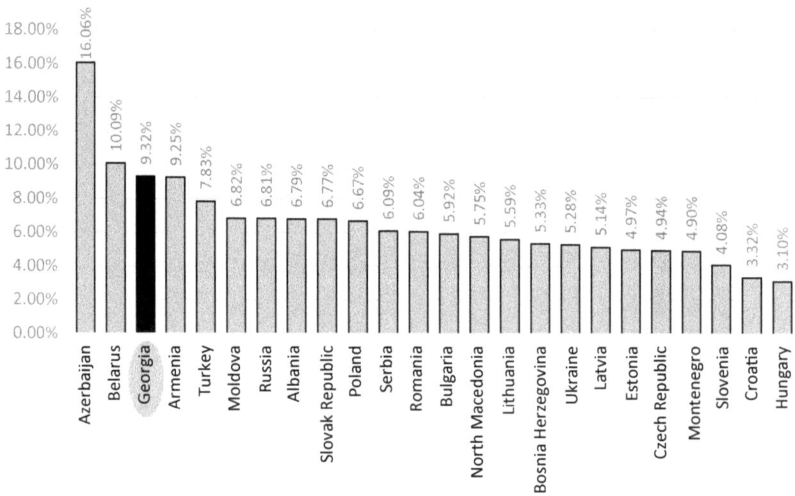

Fig. 1.3 CAGR, GDP growth in 2004–2012 (current prices, PPP, international dollars) (*Source* International Monetary Fund. World Economic Outlook databse [October 2020])

qualities is at best inefficient and in the worst-case dangerous. The narrative is intentionally maximalist. It provides a thought framework and a ranking scale for assessing capabilities of public leaders.

Chapter 7 discusses ten pillars of the state building: leadership, national memory and objectives, sense of urgency and independent thinking, individual and collective risk-taking, political consolidation, law and order, national security, public institutions and services, personal integrity, management of public expectations and strategic communication. The narrative is Georgia-specific, although it might help elsewhere. Main takeaways: the state building stalls unless it rests on these ten pillars; all pillars are important—an ecosystem of the state building is only as strong as its weakest link.

Chapter 8 alerts to futility of individual reforms (irrespective of how well intentioned and well designed these might be) in the context of a bad national governance. What are people-level implications of a bad national governance? Is there a way back from bad to good governance? Why is it crucial to act on early warning signs?

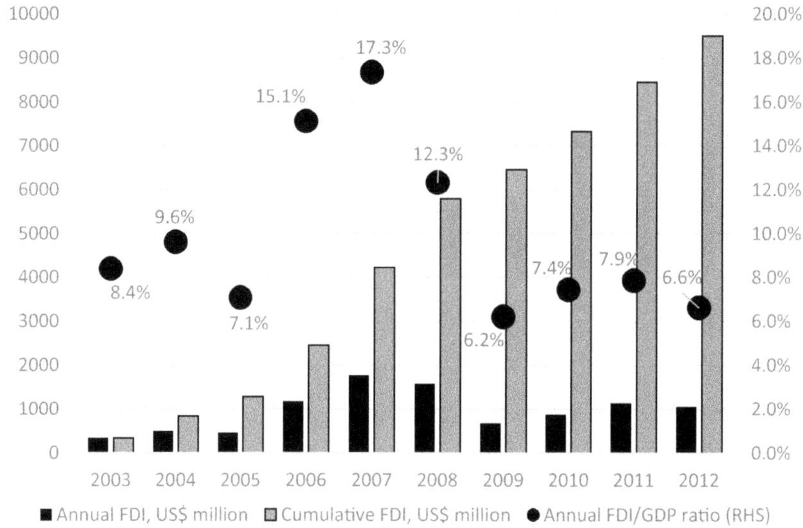

Fig. 1.4 Annual and cumulative FDI to Georgia in 2003–2012[5] (*Source* Geostat [May 2020]; International Monetary Fund, World Economic Outlook databse [October 2019])

Chapters 9–16 explain Georgia's economic history of 2004–2012—the economic dimension of the state building. The chapters are both Georgia-specific and general, with cross-country comparisons and take-aways for developing countries. They are centered around policies which (1) were, on balance, under the purview of the government, i.e., public action directly influenced end-results, (2) were cross-sectoral in their impact and nature and (3) catalyzed downstream sectoral and institutional transformations. What is the proper size, structure and raison d'être of a government? What is the relationship between a government size,

[5] In 2004–2012, Georgia attracted almost US$ 10 billion of a geographically-diversified FDI. Of total FDI in 2004–2012, 11% came from the UK, 9% each from the Netherlands and Turkey, 8% from the United States, 7% from the UAE, 6% each from Azerbaijan and Virgin Islands, 4% each from the Czech Republic, Russia, Cyprus and Germany, 3% each from Denmark, Kazakhstan and international organisations. The remaining 20% of the total FDI which Georgia received in 2004–2012 relates to 59 countries and jurisdictions. In this FDI push, all layers of the government acted as one consolidated investor relations machine.

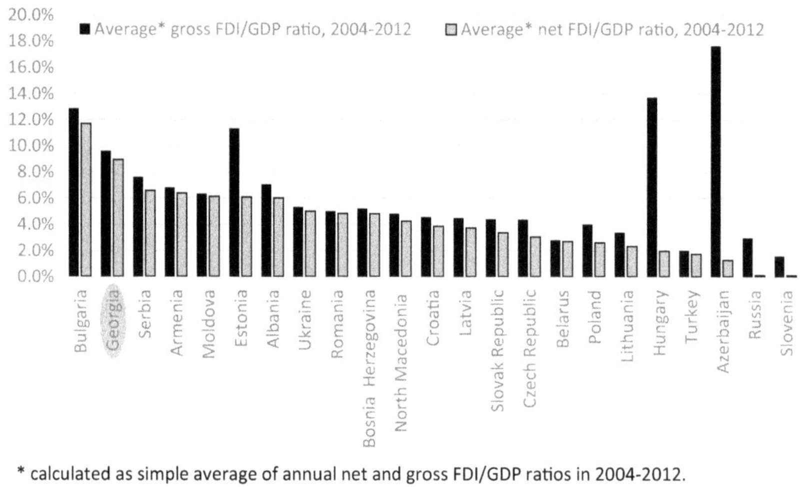

Fig. 1.5 Average inbound net and gross FDI/GDP ratios in 2004–2012 (listed by net FDI/GDP ratio, largest to smallest) (*Source* International Monetary Fund, Datamapper for both FDI statistics and GDP [retrieved from https://www.imf.org/external/datamapper/DirectIn@CF/SPR_LIDC in April 2021])

government effectiveness and economic growth? What is the optimum composition of public spending? What is the best split between a recurrent and infrastructure spending and how is it related to the resilience of public finances? Which public infrastructure schemes trigger highest positive multipliers? What are the risks inherent in public-private partnership (PPP) schemes and under which circumstances do PPPs work? How to preclude contingent liabilities through minimization of the role of state banks and of state-owned enterprises? Is there a relationship between budget deficit and growth? How and why to avoid the emergence of a premature welfare state through proper conceptualization of social spending? How to think of a market-based approach to agricultural development and healthcare? To what extent is growth and employment in these sectors correlated with public spending? Which pension systems work at a low- to middle-income level and which factors to consider? How to best incentivize civil servants? What is the role of public salaries? Which legal, procedural and institutional safeguards help to manage public debt

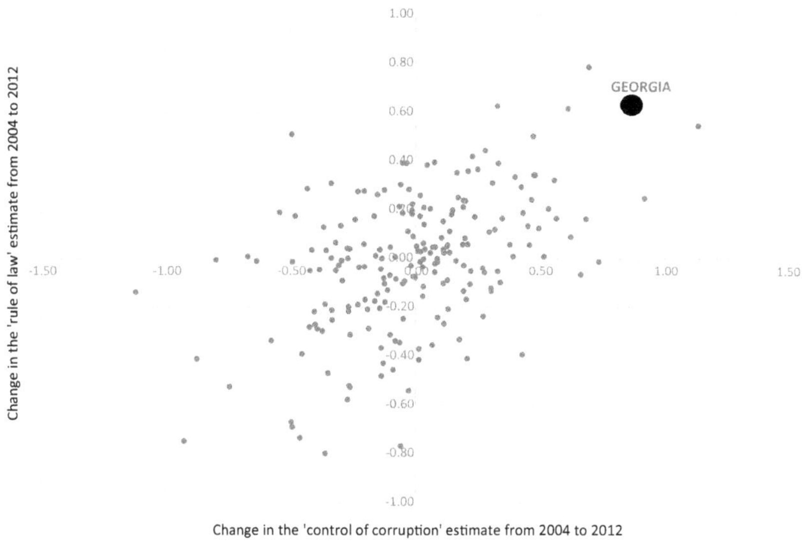

* Reflects perceptions of the extent to which public power is exercised for private gain, including both petty and grand forms of corruption, as well as "capture" of the state by elites and private interests.
** Reflects perceptions of the extent to which agents have confidence in and abide by the rules of society, and in particular the quality of contract enforcement, property rights, the police, and the courts, as well as the likelihood of crime and violence.

Fig. 1.6 Georgia—the highest improvement in the "control of corruption" * and in the "rule of law" ** estimates in 2004–2012 (global dataset, higher figure means improvement) (*Source* The World Bank. Worldwide Governance Indicators)

properly? How to measure public debt sustainability in developing countries? What are the benefits and risks inherent in the access to international capital markets? How to best benefit from a donor assistance? Who creates wealth? Why are supply-side (structural) economic measures important for wealth creation? Why is successful tax reform much more than a reduction in the number of taxes and in tax rates? Which customs and trade liberalization, transportation, deregulation, privatization, competition and public services innovation policies to adopt and how do these policies supplement each other? Which are political, technical, institutional and procedural tenets of a modern, profitable and stable banking sector? Chapters 9–16 provide qualitative and quantitative insights.

Chapter 17 explains how spatial planning, connectivity and urban regeneration can foster employment and growth. It discusses transformation of Georgia's territorial development after the Soviet break-up and details what I think were the principles behind Georgia's territorial development and urbanization in 2004–2012: (1) foresight, adaptability and boldness, (2) livability of Tbilisi through harnessing of its uniqueness, creating landmarks and addressing over-congestion, (3) mitigation of Tbilisi's over-dominance through development of other cities and regions, and (4) coastal development.

Chapter 18 explains whether and under which conditions Georgia can benefit from adoption of EUR or US$ as its sole legal tender. This triggers a discussion of common currency areas, of trade-offs between exchange rates, financial openness, and monetary independence, of transaction costs of international trade, of trade-offs between nominal and internal devaluation, etc.

Chapter 19 discusses the parliamentary elections of 2012—complex historic, social, emotional, economic, political and geopolitical reasons behind its outcome. Beware those who discard this complexity and embrace simplistic verdicts. Retrospective and/or remote observation is easier than handling complex real-time challenges of which Georgia of 2004–2012 saw many. The chapter's important message: national transformation is a marathon run where the legacy is built across multiple electoral cycles.

Chapter 20 puts things into perspective, explaining growth scenarios under which Georgia can catch up with high-income economies. The path of such convergence is difficult. It depends on domestic and external factors stretching beyond the realm of the economics. Social contracts are not static. What is good at one stage of development might become less relevant afterward.

This book comprises cross-country comparisons and abstract thoughts. But in its core it is about Georgia. My views on the state building are mainly Georgia-related.

Views expressed in this book are entirely my own and do not represent views of any of my employers.

CHAPTER 2

The Soviet Union—The Twilight

Abstract In this chapter, I share own experience of living in the Soviet Union. The chapter explains why the Soviet Union disintegrated in 1991, leaving in its wake severe governance challenges, poverty, corruption, mismanagement, distrust, emigration, crime, conflicts, defunct economic systems and institutions and disoriented citizens.

Keywords Soviet Union · Perestroika · Gorbachev · Independence

I was 13 years old when the US President Ronald Reagan and the Soviet leader Mikhail Gorbachev met at the Reykjavík summit in October of 1986. Ronald Reagan was the first US President I could recall. I sensed that something significant was in the air when my barber in Tbilisi glued to his mirror station a photo of Mr. Reagan and Mr. Gorbachev shaking hands after their meeting at Hofdi House. The Soviet Union then imploded in 1991, leading to the breakneck post-Soviet transition. Georgia exfiltrated itself from the communism and plunged into the vortex of the 1990s.

Memories of my generation cut through three periods: (1) last years of the Soviet Union, (2) the post-Soviet freefall and confusion in the first half of the 1990s and relative stabilization in 1995–2003 and (3) Georgia after the Revolution of Roses of November 2003. The more distant the period,

D. Gvindadze, *The Transformation of Georgia from 2004 to 2012*,
https://doi.org/10.1007/978-3-031-18264-8_2

the sketchier the memories. This chapter presents my own recollection of the Soviet twilight.

One of the fifteen constituent republics of the Soviet Union, Georgia preserved its culture and traditions. People spoke Georgian and knew their history. Good climate, tasty cuisine, hospitality, rich natural and cultural heritage, summer and winter opportunities attracted thousands of tourists from the "Communist Block" and beyond. Georgia's theater, dance, cinema and music were famous throughout the Soviet space. Georgians were not devout communists—the party membership was mainly the way to advance a career.

Mr. Gorbachev's Perestroika launched in 1985 introduced market reforms and exposed the lack of the consumer choice in the Soviet Union. American jeans (the Montana jeans with many zips and stickers were the first to descend upon us), chewing gum with nice etiquettes and imported ballpoint pens were atop of everyone's dream list. Teenagers started collecting chewing gum wraps featuring colors brighter than anything the Soviet reality of the time could offer.

Privileged few who in the Soviet times traveled abroad under a watchful eye of the KGB spoke profusely about department stores and about the versatility of consumer items and architectural solutions. Even the "Communist Block" countries like Yugoslavia and Eastern Germany which had been dragging behind countries on the other side of the Iron Curtain triggered envy.

Soviet passenger cars were produced mainly in Russia. Even when you could pay you had to sign up and wait for months or years. For fear of being noticed, those able to afford Volgas were buying smaller and cheaper Zhigulis. Black Volgas were used mainly by high ranking officials.

As a school kid, I was collecting small model cars sold in several shops in Georgia's capital Tbilisi. My collection was missing one car—a sports-style Moskvytch with stickers on it. I could not locate it anywhere. Walking after school past a hotel in Tbilisi (Intourist hotel hosting foreigners, which entailed KGB presence), I stumbled into such model car staring at me from a shelf inside the hotel lobby. I could not enter and kept gazing through the glass. An English-speaking man helped me in and I bought the toy. Parents were soon notified of my misbehavior.

The word "import" had a majestic connotation. To secure a foreign coat, shoes or furniture, those who could afford it were ready to overpay to wheeler-dealers who were smuggling these items in or buying them secretly from outlets serving the government nomenklatura. The law enforcement knew and was probably involved. Wheeler-dealers were selling imported medicines at significant profit margins. Some items were brought to organizations in limited numbers and people were casting lots. Personal connection to a shop or a warehouse administrator was key to securing imported items.

Some parents were going an extra mile buying for their kids school uniforms and notebooks produced in Moscow. They would ask a friend or a relative traveling to Moscow to bring these to Tbilisi. Such notebooks were glossier and uniforms had nice signs of an open book on right sleeves of jackets. At the age of eleven or twelve, I proudly entered the school building in Puma sneakers sold by a friendly warehouse administrator. That same morning, the school divided boys into teams and dispatched them to collect scrap metal from the neighborhood—old cast iron heating batteries, rusty corrugated metal plates, fences, armature, etc. By early afternoon, school yard was full of iron. The scrap gathering had a patriotic undertone. My shoes were rusty brown and torn apart.

Two small government-run retail shops in Tbilisi sold revered imported items: stereo cassette recorders (with multiple sound equalizers!) and other electronic and kitchen accessories. These shops targeted Soviet citizens who earned incomes in hard currency, mostly abroad. This hard currency was then converted into special "checks" used as the medium of exchange in these two shops. Possession of the hard currency by Soviet citizens was forbidden (those visiting capitalist countries were allowed to have a very limited number of pounds or dollars). Not without a risk, some owners of the "checks" were exchanging their "checks" back into hard currencies on the black market.

Managers of industrial plants and factories boasted about their prowess in securing supplies of raw materials and equipment from other Soviet republics. Plants and factories in Georgia and in other Soviet republics had their annual production quotas set through a centralized planning to ensure seamless supply of inputs across the Soviet Union. In the reality, each plant had its "problem-solver" with a strong interpersonal and networking talent. He—it was always *he*—would be sent regularly to plants in other Soviet republics to ensure—through persisting, wining, dining and bribing—that materials and equipment were procured on time to meet the production quotas.

Allegiance to communism was mainly materialistic. Party membership helped to land a better job. By the age of 16, everyone was expected to join Komsomol (the youth division of the Communist Party). You had to stir a real trouble to be denied the progression.

Reaching pension age was the end of the road. State pensions were enough for basic medicine and food. Personal savings were meager. Sights of Western pensioners visiting Georgia in teams contrasted with Soviet pensioners who stayed put.

Television in the Soviet Georgia had three state channels. Two were broadcast from Moscow to all Soviet republics. Both were heavy on propaganda, critical of the West and reporting how people around the world were trying to emulate the Soviet path. Third channel—relatively less ideological—was Georgian. We all—irrespective of age—were longing for Saturday evenings on the Georgian channel. After news digests, we watched Otar Sepiashvili—a famous Georgian journalist, essayist and movie critic who in the beginning of the 1980s authored and anchored a weekly program "Illusion." It offered one Western movie a week, preceded by the anchor's insights into movies' context and linking movies to broader cinematographic and societal trends. The "Illusion" was a breath of fresh air at the time when the system disliked critical thinking.

More Western movies emerged from the mid-1980s when video-cassette recorders dented monopoly of the state television. Hollywood captivated. Smoke-filled video parlors popping up across Georgia started offering unabridged Western movies, attracting thousands. In 1987, in one of such parlors in Tbilisi, we watched Rocky IV in which an American boxer Rocky Balboa confronts the Soviet boxer Ivan Drago. Spirit in the room? Georgia was pro-Rocky, at the time of the Cold War which still had three-four years to go. Did we support Rocky because this was the producer's plot, or was it something else, related to a perception of the superiority of Ronald Reagan's America? For me, it was mainly the latter. Even if some in that smoke-filled room were pro-Rocky because such was the movie's intent, I cannot imagine how a similar Soviet propaganda piece could gather thousands of pro-Soviet-boxer Americans in New York of the 1980s.

By the 1980s, the Soviet economy could not compete with an increasingly agile and innovative Western enterprise. Soviet factories had been built to last for decades, catering to steady domestic and socialist markets. A "creative destruction" was never supposed to happen. With globalization boosting cross-border competition and fostering the mobility of factors of production, the marketplace was becoming global. Bureaucrats heading Soviet state-owned enterprises were expected to pursue at once political, social and industrial goals which buffeted one against another. Output was more important than profit. Shareholder value maximization was not in managers' scorecards. Except for the military-industrial complex, manufacturing was becoming outdated. Car industry was a good example. Soviet passenger cars in the 1950s–1970s were at roughly the same level—in terms of technology and design—as cars produced in the West. By the 1980s, the divide became glaring. Western car factories were churning out an increasingly broad spectrum of bodies, colors, engines, tires, upholsteries and safety features. Soviet cars persevered with almost the same old boxy designs, basic engines, noisy interiors and neglected safety features. Even supply of those boxy cars was short of demand, epitomizing failure of the central planning. American Cadillac, French Citroën or German Mercedes Benz in Tbilisi of the 1980s would attract watchers exploring these cars' exteriors and gazing through windows to appreciate interiors.

Flats and land plots were mainly distributed by employing public institutions. Locations depended on seniority of employers and on prestige of professions. "Intelligentsia"—"intellectuals who formed an artistic, social and political vanguard or elite"[1]—and administrative nomenklatura benefitted from better deals than representatives of more prosaic work streams. Singular perks to which certain professions and individuals were traditionally entitled engendered a sense of privilege, including the claimed privilege to shape public opinion. The perks also cultivated the sense of entitlement, conformism, double standards (preaching something to others while seeking a different treatment for own self), suspicion toward meritocracy, hypocrisy, inability and unwillingness to comprehend own failings. Three decades after the Soviet collapse, these "movers and shakers" of the public opinion continue to represent a collective force that cannot be ignored, including at elections.

Taxi drivers are among the best guides into their countries' past, present and future. One such taxi driver—my random interlocutor in a post-Soviet country in the 2010s—was in his early fifties, old enough to remember the Soviet twilight. I asked about his stressful Soviet experience. He worked as a foreman at a factory in the 1980s. He had a key to a warehouse, so he stole an electric motor, brought it home to sell next day. Late in the evening, his shift supervisor called, explaining that he had

[1] Merriam-Webster dictionary.

already stolen that same motor but left it in the warehouse until he would find a buyer. The supervisor explained he had zero flexibility to share the loot with the foreman because deputy manager of the factory was to receive most of the proceeds of the sale. Next morning, the foreman returned the motor to its original shelf. A bitter feeling had haunted him ever since. As the foreman-turned-taxi-driver sped up along one of central avenues, I asked him about a man staring at us from a large electoral banner. The driver's answer: "He is a good public servant, he built this road. He stole some money like others, but he built the road, so he is OK." I retorted that the man on the banner could not be a good civil servant. The driver's reaction: "yeah, I know, but you know…".

This story epitomizes the Soviet "tragedy of commons"—the term describing how pursuit of individual self-interest depletes a common good because individuals perceive their association with the common good as tangential. When something belongs to everyone, it belongs to none.

The mismatch between demand and supply forced people to waste their "heart and nerve and sinew" in queues for even basic items. Central planning meant lack of diversity: identical building designs, identical chairs, tables, book-shelves, lamps, cutlery, carpets, food and clothes. Three decades after the Soviet collapse, this sameness can still be felt when traveling in the post-Soviet space.

To buy a heart pacemaker for a parent in the 1980s, my father traveled to Moscow. Surgeons in Tbilisi shared a name of an official in Moscow where the quest for the pacemaker could start. Guided by such official's assistant, my father went to another organization and then to a warehouse. He was crisscrossing the city for two days. Assistants to officials were gatekeepers. Back in Tbilisi with the pacemaker, father shared his contacts with families of other patients on a waiting list. If the pacemaker technology existed, and if patients wanted to get it, why wouldn't an economy churning out intercontinental missiles produce enough of these devices?

Three General Secretaries of the Soviet Union who preceded Mikhail Gorbachev whose term started in 1985 died holding this top position in the Communist Party. Two of them lasted as General Secretaries for a little more than a year each. Soviet economic planning horizon spanned five years, so the Communist Party congresses were held in Moscow every five years. In 1981, at the age of seven and sick at home, I remember (strangely, I remember it) staring at the twenty-sixth congress on TV. A speech by the General Secretary of the Communist Party spanned time

between my two regular meals. That was the last pre-Mikhail Gorbachev congress. Awakening of the Central and Eastern Europe was underway. Ronald Reagan's Strategic Defence Initiative was announced in 1983 to protect the United States from long-range ballistic missiles. It shattered the doctrine of a mutually assured destruction between the United States and the Soviet Union. The initiative caused anxiety in the Soviet Union which was unable to scale up its competition with the West.

Perestroika from the late 1980s liberalized movement of people. Soviet citizens moving out were no longer perceived as potential traitors. Thousands emigrated. A narrow entrance corridor of Tbilisi's old international airport brimmed with people holding big bags. Tears were aplenty and emotions ran high. Left behind were relatives, neighbors and friends. International mobility at that time was a privilege, so the odds of reconnecting were unclear.

Friends from Ukraine were visiting us regularly. They travelled by car from Eastern Ukraine to Tbilisi—a two-day journey. At the end of the 1980s, when Georgia experienced economic hardship, their car was full of candies, sausages and canned food produced in Ukraine. Ukraine's large size, industrial potential, location and absence of wars before and after the Soviet break-up made it luckier than Georgia in those years. From 2014, these friends live in a tragedy that Russia's war on Ukraine has created.

I received my first university stipend in Tbilisi in September of 1990. Monthly stipends were paid to all students. They were small—a local equivalent of 10–15 US dollars. At the age of sixteen, this was the first time we would get own money. Some thirty of us—the entire class—went to an administrative building of the university and waited until a cashier handed out a pack of cash through a small window. Soviet rubles were in circulation until 1993. We were to divide the pack in equal shares. Immediately, we were approached by lads in their mid-twenties. After a tense exchange which came close to a group fight, we got away with it. Stipends remained in our pockets. Several of us went to a restaurant at a hotel in the center of Tbilisi. An hour into the dinner, we were approached by two men in suits, probably a vice squad. Adding insult to the injury of that day, they said that we were young for a restaurant and that we were sitting close to foreigners. We were shifted to an empty far end of the room. A dinner in an Intourist-class hotel was not supposed to be a routine exercise.

Memories of representatives of an older generation who managed Soviet shops, factories and anything else lead to a conclusion that corruption was ubiquitous. The Soviet economy depended on backdoor deals, opportunism, risk-taking, collusion with police and prosecution and fake invoicing. Plant and factory managers walked a tightrope to avoid prisons and fines. They developed a strong *esprit de corps*, forming a close-knit network of mutual responsibilities and complicities. Ask them to explain the essence of their work and the likely answer would be—if you wanted to live you had to spin. "Spin" meant a prowess in duping the "system." The word "system" here transcended Georgia; it related to the entire Soviet Union.

The Soviet-Afghan War of 1979–1989 contributed to the Soviet demise. Georgians abhorred Soviet proxy fights of the Cold War. To avoid military service in Afghanistan, and to mitigate the risk of returning to Georgia in a zinc coffin, people spared no means and methods. One way to avoid the military service in Afghanistan as a teenager was to get admission to a university. Bribery at entrance examinations was widespread.[2] Writing their university admission tests, school graduates thus bore in mind the risk of them confronting mujahedeen in case of a failure to secure a university seat. The prospects of Georgian teenagers spending two years in a Soviet military in the Soviet Far East or in Siberia were likewise unappealing. Newcomers—"salagi"—were routinely harassed by "stariki"—soldiers at the end of their regular military service, with ethnic factors influencing the dynamics of mutual abuse.

English-language magazines and newspapers started appearing from the end of the 1980s. Many were translated into Russian. American and European magazines and fashion catalogues were immensely more versatile and colorful than the Soviet publications.

The "Searchlight of Perestroïka"—a prime time analytical daily broadcast from Moscow in 1987–1989—exposed clumsiness of the Soviet system. Its "managed candidness" approach was conceived to help implement Mikhail Gorbachev's incremental reforms. Instead, it unleashed self-criticism and self-doubt which shattered the Soviet ideology.

By the end of the 1980s, anti-Soviet movement in the then Soviet Georgia gained pace. On 9 April 1989, a pro-independence rally in Tbilisi

[2] This corruption was rooted out after 2005 when university admission decisions shifted from universities to a centralized admission system administered by the National Examination Centre.

gathered thousands. Georgia's Communist leadership was in disarray. Soviet military attacked to restore order. Use of chemical substances, military spades and batons was ruthless. Chase of unarmed protesters resulted in mass injuries and 21 deaths, including many women. Soviet army imposed a curfew. A tank in my neighborhood occasionally rotated its gun to push away neighbors who tried to instill sanity into the Soviet soldiers. At night, tanks roared back and forth along central avenues. The government of the Georgian Soviet Socialist Republic resigned. Strikes and mourning ensued. Georgia became the epicenter of de-Sovietisation. In 1989, thousands of Estonians, Latvians and Lithuanians stood in a human chain across the Baltic states to protest against spheres of influence in Europe and occupation of the Baltic states in 1940. This imbued everyone in Georgia with a feeling of proximity with Estonia, Latvia and Lithuania. In two years, on 9 April 1991, Georgia declared its independence from the Soviet Union. This restored the 1918–1921 Georgian sovereign state which had ended with the Soviet occupation of Georgia in 1921.

In December of 1991, leaders of Russia, Ukraine and Belarus dissolved the Soviet Union and established a looser formation—the Commonwealth of Independent States (CIS). Out of fifteen ex-Soviet republics, four—Estonia, Georgia, Latvia and Lithuania—did not join. The three Baltic states soon joined the EU and NATO, which fostered their development. Georgia was forced to join the CIS in December of 1993 under pressure from Moscow which supported separatism in Georgia's regions of Abkhazia and Samachablo (South Ossetia). Georgia left the CIS after Russia invaded Georgia in 2008.

By the time Mr. Gorbachev became General Secretary of the Communist Party of the Soviet Union in 1985, the country was a terminally ill patient. In 1990–1991, when Mr. Gorbachev was President of the Soviet Union, the patient was on its death bed. Mr. Gorbachev performed a euthanasia.

Terminal illness cannot explain all qualities of a patient. The Soviet Union had its scientific, educational and infrastructural achievements. But it was failed by its life-critical functions. It disintegrated despite all military, industrial, trade, linguistic, historical, geographic, infrastructural, administrative, criminal and intelligence-related networks among the fifteen Soviet republics.

Whisperers of a sterilized narrative of the Soviet past—including those nostalgic about their young years, those lamenting their lost privileges and those proud of duping the Communist system—must think deeper about why the Soviet Union disintegrated, leaving in its wake poverty, distrust, emigration, wars, defunct economic systems and institutions, disoriented and demoralized citizens and severe national governance challenges.

CHAPTER 3

1991–2003: Early Post-soviet Transition and the Revolution of Roses

Abstract This chapter explains Georgia's early post-Soviet transition—its human, social, economic, political and geopolitical aspects. It explains the peaceful Revolution of Roses in November of 2003—the first street-led revolution of the post-Soviet era.

Keywords Gamsakhurdia · Shevardnadze · Saakashvili · Revolution of Roses

Georgia's early post-Soviet transition to sovereignty and to market economy was difficult. Fighting against the Russia-inspired, Russia-backed and Russia-armed separatism in Abkhazia and in Samachablo (South Ossetia) in the beginning of the 1990s resulted in loss of the de facto control over much of these territories, in refugees and in more than 300,000 internally displaced persons. Tragedies and traumas of those years continue to impair Georgia's path of development. Echoes of those tragedies and traumas define everything and everyone in Georgia to this day.

Regional instability of the early 1990s hit business confidence. Disruption of economic networks led to abrupt shifts in Georgia's trade and energy consumption arrangements (in the Soviet times, Georgia's trade had been mainly an inter-republican trade within the Soviet Union which

D. Gvindadze, *The Transformation of Georgia from 2004 to 2012*,
https://doi.org/10.1007/978-3-031-18264-8_3

depended on transport routes to Russia and on established payment channels). Disappearance of the old Soviet banking system and hyperinflation of the first half of the 1990s destroyed deposit savings. Tax revenues' share in GDP dropped to single digits and fiscal deficits skyrocketed to more than 20% in 1992–1993, funded by external grants and loans and by the central bank. Increases in the central bank's lending in coupons (coupon was a temporary unit of account in 1993–1995 before introduction of the Georgian Lari) were followed by conversion of coupons into US dollars, leading to a depletion of the central bank's foreign reserves and to coupon's fast devaluation fueling high inflation. The government transacted in coupons, but Russian rubles and hard currencies underpinned a much larger volume of transactions.

A coup d'etat against Georgia's first democratically elected President Zviad Gamsakhurdia turned violent at the end of 1991. It turned the center of Tbilisi into a warzone and mutated into a protracted unrest which weakened Georgia at the time when the mentioned separatist threats peaked. Mr. Gamsakhurdia's presidency lasted less than one year. He was forced to leave Georgia and died in unclear circumstances. This left scars which polarized Georgia for decades.

Georgia's second President Eduard Shevardnadze had been Soviet Minister of Foreign Affairs under President Mikhail Gorbachev. He returned to Georgia in 1992 and sought to establish a strategic regional role for the independent Georgia. Mr. Shevardnadze survived three assassination attempts: (1) a car bomb in Abkhazia in 1992, (2) a car bomb which exploded in the backyard of the parliament in Tbilisi in 1995 and (3) an ambush on the presidential motorcade in 1998 where the fighting was so fierce that it could be heard kilometers away. Armored Mercedes Benz saved Mr. Shevardnadze from grenade launchers and machine guns.

The early post-Soviet Caucasus was not on investors' radars. Local norms, political and administrative culture were unprepared for the new realities. Engineers and scholars became street traders. Entrepreneurs were learning the basics of the capitalism. Professional skills were missing. Disruption of the Soviet-era industrial integration hit supply chains. Many state enterprises were asset stripped and sold. Public finances were in disarray and public salaries were almost zero. Poverty skyrocketed. The wars of the 1990s resulted in deaths, stress disorders and incapacitation. Law enforcement almost broke down. Energy sector was unable to supply electricity beyond irregular intervals. A regional strongman in Georgia's Ajara region built his own fief and minimized contacts with

Tbilisi. National security infrastructure was porous. In the absence of public transport, people were hanging on back ladders of overcrowded trolley buses to move around cities at risk of being electrocuted. To buy bread in the beginning of the 1990s, people stood in exasperating queues. Places in such queues had to be reserved in the evening to get two–three loafs in the morning. Trade with Turkey—where Georgians traveled to Turkey's provinces to work, sell household items and electric appliances, buy Turkish clothes and sell them upon return to Georgia—gained vast dimensions. In the absence of proper banking, Ponzi schemes emerged where high yields in the first months were followed by bankruptcies.

The disorder and confusion spilled over into classrooms. Sitting in university auditoriums in winter in coats because of bruised windows and seeing a chosen profession becoming redundant became a common experience. The war in Abkhazia in 1992–1993 was producing dreadful daily reminders—photos of killed students glued to pillars in the main entry hall of my university. Street brawls and other risks diverted attention away from auditoriums. Student backpacks gave way to thin zipped folder bags, which students soon started folding in the middle to hold under belts. The vortex of the 1990s disoriented or criminalized many representatives of that generation. For too many, a criminal route was not a deliberate choice—they were forced into it by the circumstances. Upon graduation, classmates split in various directions, with only a few loyal to their original career tracks. Quality of education and discipline took a hit. Study became peripheral as survival priorities moved to the mainstream.

Thousands engaged in street commerce, so shops could not accommodate them. Sidewalks and underground passages became occupied by people selling family possessions. Makeshift counters and kiosks mushroomed. To push back against racketeers, some sought protection from neighborhood criminals in exchange for cash and in-kind payments. Owners of kiosks selling foreign cigarettes, liquors and candies dealt with good and bad people coming in an unpredictable order and leaving with unpredictable outcomes.

Many became taxi drivers. The lucky ones parked and waited for clients in crowded places. They served clients without consuming too much fuel. Those who were late to secure their parking places drove non-stop. Taxi drivers of the 1990s had to cope with scoundrels. With the onset of darkness, their families were waiting with trepidation for the return of their breadwinners. With no mobiles, time of such return was anyone's guess. The COB ("close of business", usually 6 pm) did not mean much for those standing in long queues for frozen chicken, fish, meat and cans of marinated sprats or herring.

Criminality increased due to the poverty, confusion, wars and the post-traumatic stress disorders. From dusk till dawn, some streets were less safe. Nighttime police ambushes which aimed at searching random cars for drugs and weapons led to routine shootouts. Possession of firearms increased. Part of new year celebrations was watching the skyline lit up with machine gun cannonades. Drivers kept metal pipes or tire irons beneath their seats for self-protection. Anyone in Georgia has relatives, friends or neighbors who in the 1990s perished in the wars or succumbed to brawls, drugs and joblessness. Cemeteries added many tombs of young people. Survivors roamed, mentally scarred and socially disoriented, Georgia's towns and villages.

Those who parked cars in yards of multi-apartment buildings and in streets performed ritual evening checks from their balconies. At dawn, some realized that car tires were removed or side mirrors were missing. To protect front and rear windshields, car owners engraved onto them vehicle identification numbers. Protecting hoods and trunks were iron rods cemented into ground from front and back of cars. Such protection sometimes invited more muscular outcomes: removal of accumulators by twisting hoods. A couple of car owners in Tbilisi of the early 1990s took protection of their cars to extremes, lifting cars to their balconies. Those whose cars were stolen pursued a twin strategy: (1) declare the theft to a police and (2) go to a criminal boss handling the neighborhood. Method (2) often worked at least as efficiently as method (1). Toward the end of the 1990s, many replaced the iron rods with garages. These were illegal metal structures which mutilated yards beyond recognition. [These illegal garages were removed by the authorities soon after the Revolution of Roses in 2003. First, people were angry, fearing the resumption of car thefts. Except that nothing bad happened. Thefts were brought down to zero on the back of the police reform from 2004 explained later in this book].

Criminal police was ruthless and weak at the same time—mistreating some and in cahoots with and/or fearing others. National security agencies lacked experience and resolve to purge infiltration in their own ranks. Traffic police—the most visible category of policing due to its proximity to people—generated disdain. Hidden behind blind turns and tree trunks, with black-and-white traffic sticks, traffic policemen hunted for cash. This cash then trickled up to feed higher echelons. The men with traffic sticks were victims and villains at the same time. To alert each other of hiding traffic policemen, drivers developed a warning sign—a double pull of a headlights switch. In words of a former traffic policeman turned taxi driver after he was laid off during police reforms after the Revolution of Roses, "everyone hated me, I also hated myself and the system, but I was at the bottom of the food chain."

No heating and irregular electricity supply in the 1990s meant that temperatures inside and outside of public buildings in winter were roughly the same. Even then, staying indoors in coats and with low salaries, thousands of public servants worked tirelessly, building an independent Georgia and laying the groundwork for its pro-Western orientation. (Hence a general takeaway: unless a public administration is hopelessly incompetent or corrupt, a change of management and of the spirit of public leadership can channel knowledge and zeal of civil servants in the right direction.)

Measurement of Georgia's economic downfall in the early 1990s is not helped by (1) dearth of a reliable statistical data for periods preceding and following the Soviet break-up in 1991 and (2) a hyperinflation which followed the transition from the Soviet rubles to coupons before introduction of the Georgian Lari (GEL) as the permanent currency in 1995. The economic downfall was significant. Real GDP in 1994 stood at one-third of its 1990 level. In four years, Georgia lost two-thirds of its economic output. Growth restarted from 1995, from the very low level (see Chapter 4 for details). Still, unlike in Russia where sentiment changed from the West enjoying popularity early in the 1990s to people blaming the West for poverty and other post-Soviet setbacks, the mood in Georgia remained staunchly pro-Western.

Despite all its problems, Georgia of 2003 was much better than Georgia of the 1990s. Strategic pipelines from Azerbaijan via Georgia to the Black Sea and to Turkey were agreed and their construction started, bringing investment and reinforcing Georgia's pro-Western orientation. Trade patterns and economic structure adjusted to the new realities. Institutions malfunctioned but were learning by doing. Crime levels dropped. People adjusted to the market economy—some embraced it and others were forced into it. Georgia of 2003 was a fragile and inexperienced country which survived despite huge external challenges and domestic mistakes. President Eduard Shevardnadze was an internationally respected statesman who had contributed to tearing down the Berlin Wall. Georgia's pro-Western orientation was genuine. Unlike post-Communist countries in Central and Eastern Europe which benefitted from time-bound paths to the European and the Euro-Atlantic integration, Georgia navigated without strong external anchors. Still, stagnation, corruption and nepotism became a permanent fixture in lives of too many. This created a fertile ground for a change.

This change—the Revolution of Roses—came in November of 2003, paving way to Georgia's transformation explained in this book. This was the first street-led revolution of the post-Soviet era. It raised hopes and sent ripples across the post-Soviet geography. It also rang alarm bells in Moscow.

The revolution was peaceful because popular support was overwhelming, the incumbent leadership stepped back and the law enforcement was weak and disoriented. After President Shevardnadze agreed to exit, the leader of the Revolution of Roses Mikheil Saakashvili said something that, in retrospect, became one of the highlights of his political career: "President Shevardnadze took a very honourable decision to resign to preserve stability in the country. President [Shevardnadze] should stay in the country. It is the matter of national dignity that Georgia's former president remains in his country, has his security fully assured, his living conditions fully guaranteed and his family protected. This is our very important task…".

The Revolution of Roses was sparked by: (1) parliamentary elections which fell short of international standards, (2) sense of injustice, (3) critical institutional and sectoral challenges (fiasco in the energy sector, dilapidated infrastructure, poverty, dismal approval rating of law enforcement agencies, unreformed and corrupt public services) and (4) economic hardship (Georgia restructured its public debt in the Paris Club in 2001 and 2004; according to the IMF notice of 7 November 2003, "…pervasive corruption and tax evasion remain(ed) the most serious obstacles to fiscal sustainability and private sector development").

I watched the Revolution of Roses from Cambridge, Massachusetts. I flew to the United States in summer of 2003. The Harvard Kennedy School admitted me to a two-year Master's program and the United States' State Department's Edmund S. Muskie Graduate Fellowship Program covered all costs. In those years, many Georgians benefitted from study fellowships from the United States and the European Union countries. Internet in my student dorm was slow. It was a pre-smartphone era. To place an international call, I was scratching off multi-digit numbers from prepaid cards and dialing them on my Nokia handset. As crowds gathered in Tbilisi in November of 2003, I was scratching off those numbers increasingly often and watching a low-bandwidth live stream on my computer. When the Revolution of Roses started, the website crashed. Nokia proved more reliable.

When I returned to Georgia in 2005, the national flag, coat of arms, anthem and other things changed. Flying next to the Georgian flag in front of the parliament was the flag of Europe hoisted by President Saakashvili on the day of his inauguration in January 2004. Many in Georgia's post-revolutionary public service were the Muskie program graduates. Some dubbed the revolution the "Muskie Revolution."

CHAPTER 4

Georgia's J-Curve. How to Rebound?

Abstract This chapter discusses Georgia's economic fall in 1990–1995 and compares it to other post-Soviet countries. It explains Georgia's relative stabilization in 1996–2003, challenges of those years and how they influenced Georgia's state building from 2004. The chapter provides general takeaways on modernization of developing countries.

Keywords Economic contraction · Stabilization · GDP · Wealth · Modernization

Georgia's economy hit the bottom in 1994–1995, four years after the declaration of independence from the Soviet Union in 1991. In the first half of the 1990s, Georgia suffered one of the deepest economic contractions on record. In real terms, Georgia's GDP in 1995 stood at

D. Gvindadze, *The Transformation of Georgia from 2004 to 2012*,
https://doi.org/10.1007/978-3-031-18264-8_4

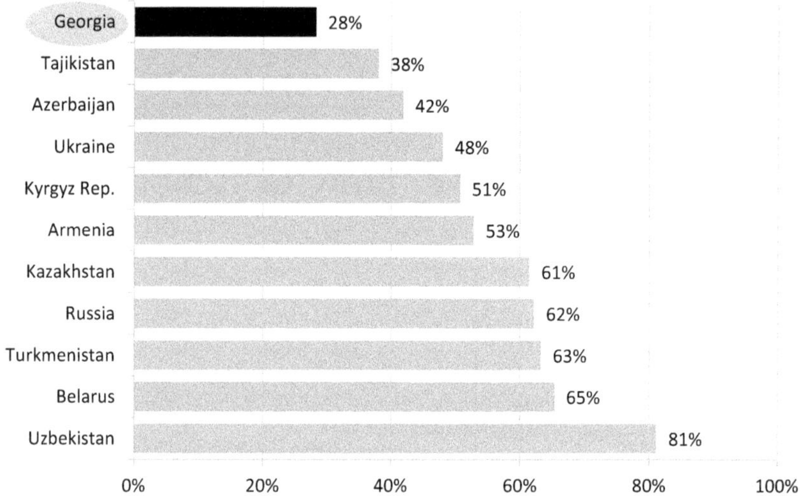

Fig. 4.1 Real output (GDP at constant prices) in 1995 compared to 1990[3] (*Source* The world bank. World Development Indicators [October 2019])

approximately 28% of the GDP in 1990.[1] This was the deepest contraction among the post-Soviet republics (Fig. 4.1). In the decade after 1994, Georgia's population shrank by one million people—20% of Georgia's population in 1991.[2]

To put things into perspective: the peak-to-trough real GDP decrease was (1) approximately 30% in the United States during the 1929 Great Depression, (2) close to 20% during the 2001 economic and financial

[1] Growth or contraction of a *real* GDP explains whether total *output (volume)* of goods and services produced in an economy is growing or shrinking. GDP is collected at nominal (current) prices, so to convert nominal GDP to real GDP in a given year economists use a deflator which allows to adjust GDP from nominal to constant prices. The 72% decline in Georgia's *real* GDP in 1990–1995 thus means that the *volume* of production decreased by 72%. This is different from a nominal GDP dynamics which reflects a volume of production *and* a price dynamics.

[2] The World Bank and Geostat (Georgian statistical agency) databases.

[3] For Georgia, mostly excludes Georgia's regions of Abkhazia and South Ossetia. Note statistical data quality challenges immediately before and after the Soviet collapse in 1991; this might have interfered with exact numbers (which are subject to regular adjustments), although not with the approximate scale of the GDP contractions in 1990--1995.

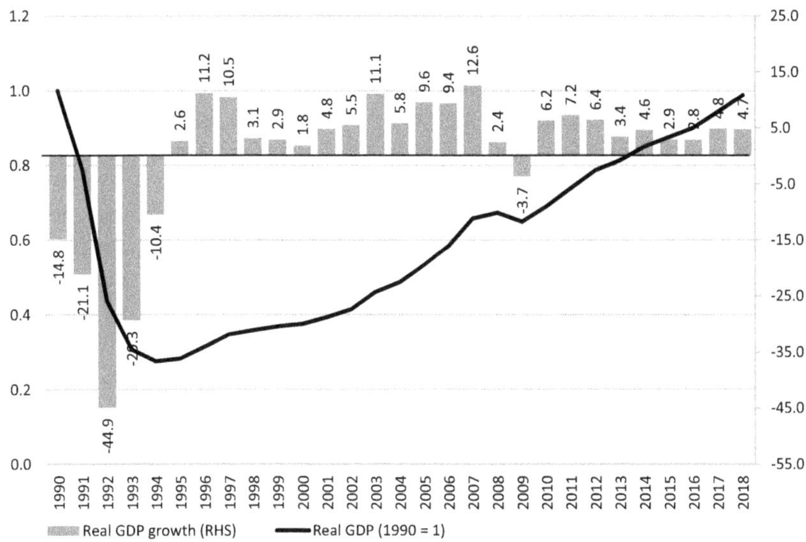

Fig. 4.2 Georgia's real GDP in 1990–2018: level and pattern (*Source* The world bank. World Development Indicators [October 2019])

crisis in Argentina and (3) up to 10–15% in Indonesia, Thailand and Malaysia during the 1997 Asian financial crisis.[4]

Notwithstanding the economic stabilization and growth from the second half of the 1990s, and growth in 2004–2012 explained in this book, Georgia's real volume of economic output in 2012 stood at approximately 80% of its 1990 level. Volume of the output climbed back to its 1990 level in 2018, after almost three decades of transition (Fig. 4.2). A close look at the economic contraction of 1990–1994 points to its broad cross-sectoral nature.

This had three main implications for Georgia in 2004–2012:

1. **To catch up with advanced countries, Georgia had to grow fast.** At approximately US$ 1,000 in 2003 (US$ 4,400 in 2012), Georgia's GDP per capita was lower than in Central Europe and much lower than in the Euro Area. The convergence could only

[4] C. Reinhart, K. Rogoff (2009).

materialize through a sustainably high growth. A real mitigation of poverty could happen through policies promoting the equality of opportunity more than the equality of outcome (no premature "welfare state"). Private entrepreneurship and investment had to be at the core of the growth strategy, although state activism was essential for strengthening of the national security, modernization of infrastructure and institutions and attracting international capital.

2. **Georgia's transformation was to take place in the context of the materialized political, economic and geopolitical risks which disrupted income, wealth and occupational patterns.** An abruptly emerged mismatch between a *stock of wealth* (a sum of tangible and intangible assets accumulated by Georgia throughout its history, including in the Soviet period) and a *flow of wealth* (GDP—an annual economic output—which tumbled in the 1990s) jeopardized a social class differentiation and increased a social and political angst. In his 1943 work "A Theory of Human Motivation," an American psychologist Abraham Maslow classified a hierarchy of human needs. This hierarchy stipulates that most of basic physiological and safety needs (food, water, warmth, rest, security, safety) must be met fully or partially before people are motivated to achieve higher-order psychological and self-fulfillment needs (belongingness and love needs, esteem needs, self-actualization). Georgia's Soviet experience and its early post-Soviet transition tied these lower- and higher-order needs into a Gordian knot, producing a behavioral storm of attitudes, allegiances, aberrations, likes and dislikes. Then, the Revolution of Roses of 2003 disrupted established practices and social hierarchies. All this influenced a threshold of intolerance to the attempted modernization and amplified fallouts from mistakes in 2004–2012.
3. **A slow change in Georgia would have only a marginal effect**. Instead, a bold strategy was to transform the nation scarred by the post-Soviet tumult, lacking modern institutions, skills, entrepreneurial spirit and critical thinking, unaccustomed to managing own fortune, taken aback by an emerged link between productivity and remuneration, prone to blaming personal failure on the government, overdependent on the state for education, housing, job security and vacations, not used to owning private property, relying on the government for the social safety net, unaware of links between individual initiative and social outcomes, prioritizing

informal practices which in the Soviet past had been as consequential as formal rules and overwhelmed by international boilerplates on how to implement the transition.[5] A book "Why Nations Fail" by Daron Acemoglu and James A. Robinson[6] explains how history—dating as far back as early resettlement and colonization in America and ancient civilizations—defines patters of the economic growth and institutional and structural divergence between, say, the United States and Mexico today. Centuries of history triggering different outcomes in closeby geographic locations. Bearing in mind Georgia's history, a breakthrough from 2004 was only possible through a path-independent change.

This leads to more general takeaways on modernization of developing countries.

1. A turnaround of a firm means re-invention of its mission, restructuring of its balance sheet, overhaul of management, procedures and systems. This inflicts pain and creates resistance. A turnaround of a country is a more complex exercise. Reversions to the mean happen, through elections or otherwise. It is difficult to transform a post-Communist economy by relaxing a limited number of (binding) constraints to growth or by reforming some institutions and keeping others under a thumb. Isolated reforms, even if well intentioned and well executed, fail. Unless such reforms unfold in conducive ecosystems encapsulating all aspects of the state building, they fade away with time and under pressure from unreformed institutions. They cannot trigger positive people-level outcomes and cannot produce lasting legacies. Praise—domestic or international—is ephemeral. National reformers who want to engineer a real breakthrough must *collectively* elevate themselves to the rank of state builders.
2. Success of a reform depends on a success of related reforms. They all thrive or all frustrate. Imagine a system of communicating vessels.

[5] Many of these traits relate to the term "Homo Sovieticus" which was popularized by Alexandr Zinovyev in his novel titled Homo Sovieticus (1986) exploring the nature of a new people created by the Soviet society.

[6] D. Acemoglu and J. A. Robinson (2013).

There are two ways to fill it with a liquid: (1) pour liquid profusely into one vessel and wait for it to leak into other vessels and (2) pour smaller volumes of liquid simultaneously into all vessels. Some resource-rich economies are in the former category: hydrocarbon revenues fuel all government actions. Georgia is in the latter category. Take banking as an example. Proper regulation of the financial sector must come together with good operational and legal environment and with modern public services (public and civil registries, etc.). Demand for loans and reduction of non-performing assets depend on a political commitment to sound macroeconomic and structural economic policies which catalyze investment and preclude monopolies. Even the best legal act cannot guarantee a strong and independent central bank unless political leaders ring-fence it from domestic and transnational criminals who view banks as cash cows and laundry vehicles. This underlines the importance of the rule of law. Modern banking thus cannot materialize in an adverse political, operational, legal and institutional context. Same causal links exist in all other sectors. As explained later in this book, agricultural modernization cannot happen without dynamic retail and corporate sectors which, in turn, depend on factors influencing growth and investment in these sectors. Healthcare cannot develop without a modern insurance industry and public–private partnerships involving quality private investors. Such investors will not lock themselves in unless they do not expect policy reversals denting their long-term rates of return. Ultimately, all reforms depend on demographics, itself the by-product of domestic and external circumstances.

3. It is important to have a national development strategy, but too many strategies distract. Ask a public official in a mismanaged country to share his country's development strategy. You will soon be staring at time-bound reforms matrices, sectoral action plans and roadmaps with performance milestones and monitoring benchmarks. Expect these documents drafted in English because they represent foreign aid conditionalities. Public officials in mismanaged countries churn out resolutions, regulations, decrees and orders, and create anti-monopoly and anti-corruption entities. They often window dress. Then, governments change and national strategizing, benchmarking and milestoning exercises restart. International advisors and partners seek to relaunch stalled reforms. Reports proliferate and land on desks of public officials. Google "economic

competitiveness reforms strategy action plan country x." Even for most under-researched countries, the search engine will unearth many strategies from the past. A zeal to discover a holy grail of development through yet another strategy in countries paying a lip service to reforms cannot translate into actions. Vested interests use "reforms" to justify laws promoting their own goals. So, keep it simple, be blunt and candid!

4. An equation of national development has many variables. Such equations are algebraically unsolvable. A reformist government can directly influence some but not all variables. Starting conditions matter. Had Georgia's geopolitics been less turbulent, its domestic politics would have been less polarized. Long-term development is not only the by-product of economic policies. Non-economic enablers of the development matter. A strong statehood is positively correlated with good business climate and low corruption, but the relationship is not linear. A consolidated nation with strong, experienced and de-politicized national security institutions, but a lower score in the World Bank's Doing Business ranking might prove more resilient to domestic and external challenges than a nation with a higher "doing business" score but a porous national security establishment. Georgia is a small country in the region known for its repetitive eruptions of geopolitical testosterone. Miscalculations in any domain of the state building may eliminate value created by economic reforms. All this at the time when measures which external adversaries can deploy to influence domestic politics of small open economies located at geopolitical fault lines have become complex and treacherous. Memoirs of leaders who transformed their countries thus explain growth and development better than analyses by economists which offer narrower narratives. To build a strong nation which cannot be undone, the leadership must stretch beyond the realm of the economics.
5. Radical transformations are idiosyncratic, controversial and risky. They are best understood and implemented by visionary national state builders and they cannot be outsourced. Off-the-shelf solutions in the domain of the state building do not exist. Countries act in line with their constraints and opportunities, although a moral compass of the public leadership must be the same across geographies. Excessive reliance on "best international practice" at

the expense of domestic experimentation may proliferate a paperwork and event management. But it may not ensure convergence with high-income economies. International good will and expertise help: foreign official lenders' and donors' conditionalities support reformers in their fight against domestic detractors; diplomatic mediation might help address domestic political crises. Still, complex transformations entail handling multiple constituencies, taking political risks and connecting dots which are visible only to insiders. Big decisions are influenced by closed-door trade-offs, by financial, kinship and political ties and allegiances, by national security factors, power balances, rational and irrational feelings and traits of character which only insiders can grasp and act upon. In countries with informal leadership structures, foreigners may be talking to "front offices" (formal government appointees with good intentions but little influence), whereas back offices churn out real verdicts and decisions. This limited interaction with real power brokers may amplify information asymmetries, increase odds of misjudgment or feed "expatriate rumor mills" which misinterpret or ignore higher-order causes, effects and implications. National public officials' comprehensive engagement with the international community is pivotal for addressing the information asymmetries. In 2004–2012, Georgia had exceptional foreign friends and supporters—statesmen, politicians, diplomats, development partners—who acted on their profound understanding of Georgia's challenges. We also knew those whose bias and an insufficient understanding of the local context did not stop them from pontificating profusely. The experience with the latter category makes me very careful when discussing with a foreign government what it must and must not do.

6. Even in places where corruption and mismanagement are rampant, there are honest civil servants. The same civil servants may behave differently under different forms of leadership and national governance. A policeman reluctant to confront a criminal when a system which employs him malfunctions and exposes his family to retaliations can commit acts of valor when he serves a higher purpose, has clear orders and is personally protected and respected. A thorough overhaul of institutions, therefore, does not necessarily entail indiscriminate layoffs unless the scale of a problem requires sweeping solutions. But without a top-level political resolve, the honest civil servants cannot disrupt a status quo. An individual professional

sacrifice cannot be a game changer unless the national governance improves. Such improvement can only be engineered by heads of state, especially in developing countries with immature institutions. Civic activism and grassroots pressures can nudge governments in the right direction. Civic pressure may trigger a revolution, but without a strong and visionary public leadership a revolution cannot deliver on its promise.

7. Staunch and time-tested international allies radiating valor, audacity, determination and grand vision share the planet with detractors and laggards afflicted by mercantilism, short-termism, spinelessness, indifference, myopia and condescendence. International institutions are not immune from complex global realities which at times sanitize such institutions' discourse and constrain their action. Bilateral relations are influenced by shifting global alliances. Small states depend on the international good will, but this goodwill cannot be taken for granted. Strong and successful countries are supported and respected. They have more allies willing to defend them against enemies.
8. A skillful spin and starting conditions matter. Neglecting the spin is like running a large manufacturing operation with zero marketing budget. Starting conditions differ. Georgia's starting conditions were influenced by its transshipment and logistics potential and by agricultural and tourism franchises with significant regional brand recognition spanning many decades. Other countries border the European Union and might benefit more from the European near-shoring and cross-border manufacturing integration. They might have a location which no investor or policymaker can ignore. They might be rich in hydrocarbons or have global diasporas. Almost all countries have something unique which can be cultivated into a competitive edge. But a starting condition is just one variable in the equation of national development.
9. Fast national transformation is not risk-free even if powered by benign intentions. Strategic management of expectations, anxieties, aspirations, egos and peculiarities is key. Imagine an old car with a boxy body, with no spoilers to reduce wind resistance and enhance grip at high speeds, and with a straight-up rather than slanted windshield. Turbo charge such car's engine and the car's surfaces perpendicular to the incoming air will increase resistance, noise and friction. Insufficient grip at high speed will make the car slip

when entering abrupt turns. The turbo-charged engine thus cannot produce a result in the absence of an improved aerodynamics. In the context of the state building, this means that a top-down reform push must come hand in hand with a careful engagement and management of expectations, with caution with respect to individual mistakes and with lots of wisdom in the context of the law enforcement and administration of justice.

CHAPTER 5

Russia

Abstract This chapter explains Georgia's difficult relationship with Russia and its impact on Georgia's development. It explains why Russia invaded Georgia in 2008 and explores links between geopolitics and national governance.

Keywords Russia · War · NATO · Abkhazia · Samachablo (South Ossetia)

Summer of 1996. I was 22, diplomat at the Ministry of Foreign Affairs of Georgia, flying from Tbilisi to a conference in Central Europe. Organizers purchased an air ticket ("the cheapest available option"). In those days, we depended on organizers' ability to cover costs. Direct flights from Tbilisi to Europe were very limited. The organizers chose Moscow as the cheapest connection flight.

I landed in a Moscow Airport which served flights between Tbilisi and Moscow. From there, I had to reach the Sheremetyevo International Airport—a distance of approximately 60km by car. Taxi was expensive, so I took a bus and then a tram. I handed money to a tram conductor and asked for a ticket. He took money and said that a ticket was not necessary. At next stop, armed men in military uniforms entered from both doors and started checking tickets. I said that I paid, referring them to

D. Gvindadze, *The Transformation of Georgia from 2004 to 2012*,
https://doi.org/10.1007/978-3-031-18264-8_5

a conductor who sat two meters away. The conductor said I never did. I was escorted out of the tram. Passengers—including those who sat next to me and saw how I paid—watched silently and indifferently. This unfolded on one of Moscow's central avenues, so before long we were surrounded by pedestrians.

One armed man told me: "you got caught; now we will plant a drug into your pocket and you will either go to prison in Russia or will sell your property in Georgia to pay us off." I had a diplomatic passport and I knew Georgia's ambassador to Russia. I showed the passport and said that I was entitled to call my embassy. They refused. I had US$ 50 in my pocket and another US$ 50 in my bag. I said I had US$ 50 on me and that they could take it, the rest I was supposed to receive in Europe upon arrival. Meanwhile, a boxy yellow police van with a cage inside arrived and stopped next to the tram rail in the middle of the avenue. I proposed the US$ 50 again. The armed man eventually agreed. The amount was equal to my monthly salary. This sum proved more instrumental in pulling me out of the trouble than the Vienna Convention on Diplomatic Privileges and Immunities.

The man walked me to a nearby bus departing for the Sheremetyevo International Airport. He instructed a driver to take me for free. The bus door closed and the driver looked at me. "You've got caught, right? They operate here, targeting people from the Caucasus. Tram conductors are part of game."

The bus arrived at the Sheremetyevo Airport shortly before my flight's departure. To pass a border and a passport control, I ran. The plane took off and breathed a sigh of relief. On my way back to Georgia via Moscow, I mostly stayed at the airport hotel. An alarm reminiscent of a sound of a Soviet school siren announcing a break between classes woke me up next morning, at my request. I returned to Georgia and never visited Moscow again.

August of 2008. I was Deputy Minister of Finance of Georgia responsible for the cooperation with international development partners and for public debt management. At approximately 02:00 am on August 8, I left for the Tbilisi International Airport. Together with a colleague from the Ministry of Energy, I was flying to Frankfurt, Germany, to negotiate with KfW (German development bank) a high voltage transmission line project between Georgia and Turkey. Flights from Tbilisi to Europe were mostly departing at 3:00–5:00 am.

In those days, Georgia worked to attract investment into its hydro energy sector. Energy sector reforms from 2004 allowed to modernize regulation, enhance payment discipline, increase generation capacity and eradicate corruption. Hydropower generation in Georgia was expected to grow due to cost advantages and efforts to reduce Co2 emissions. From 2007, Georgia became net exporter of electricity on an annual basis. We were expecting export of an increasing share of generated capacity to neighboring countries.[1] The new transmission line and a back-to-back converter station were to interconnect Georgian and Turkish power networks. The project was one of the largest infrastructure investments in Georgia's history, co-financed by the European Bank for Reconstruction and Development, the European Investment Bank, German development bank KfW and the European Union. The new line was expected to increase the regional electricity trading, to crowd in investment into Georgia's new hydro power plants and to facilitate export of excess summer-time electricity to Turkey. We had worked for months to prepare this project. Key financial and technical terms were to be confirmed with the KfW in Frankfurt.

On the way to the Tbilisi Airport, I checked my phone. News from Georgia's Samachablo (South Ossetia) region was alarming.

Active fighting in Abkhazia and in South Ossetia had ended in the 1990s. Both regions had been under a de facto Russian occupation. The Revolution of Roses in 2003 (followed by the Orange Revolution in Ukraine in 2004–2005) fueled Moscow's distrust toward Georgia. Georgia's fast modernization from 2004—despite energy and trade blockades from Russia—had been making headlines across the post-Soviet space. The impulse of Georgia's democratic modernization was consequential for the entire region. Visiting Georgia in 2005, the US President George W. Bush had called Georgia "a beacon of liberty for this region and the world." The NATO Bucharest Summit in April of 2008 failed to produce Membership Action Plans (MAP) offers to Ukraine and Georgia, but its outcome was a public statement issued on behalf of the Alliance that "…Ukraine and Georgia will become members of NATO." In the early August of 2008, all this culminated in Russia's military invasion into Georgia—the first European war of the twenty-first century and Russia's first war abroad after its withdrawal from Afghanistan in 1989.

[1] Georgia's Hydropower Potential, Giving Water the Green Light (June 28, 2012), *Bank of Georgia Research*.

We were asked to complete the project negotiations in a day and return back. We arrived in Frankfurt and went to the KfW's central office. The negotiations lasted whole day. I kept staring at my phone. News from Georgia was increasingly ominous. CNN soon started live coverage.

We concluded the negotiations in the evening and early on August 9 left for the Frankfurt Airport. We handed passports to a Lufthansa representative. She read from her computer. "Georgia is a no-flight zone," she said.

Our families were in Tbilisi. We wanted to get back fast. We changed tickets, flew to Austria and from there to Yerevan, Armenia. Georgian passengers in the situation similar to ours constituted about a quarter of the flight. They were silent. Passengers from outside of the region and with a shallow understanding of the context were perplexed.

The connection flight to Yerevan took the whole day of August 9. We landed in Yerevan at midnight. A local driver took us to the Georgian border—a five-hour drive. A Georgian driver met on the other side of the border. In the morning of 10 August, I was in the office in Tbilisi where I spent months coordinating the post-war international assistance to Georgia.

Because of its small size, Georgia lacks a "strategic depth." South Ossetia (Samachablo) is close to Tbilisi—a three- to four-hour drive by a tank. Next to Samachablo is the East–West highway—the main corridor for Georgia, the South Caucasus and the Central Asia (for the latter's westbound exports). In August of 2008, proximity to the war zone made the highway temporarily dysfunctional. Russian troops passed Gori—the city 90km from Tbilisi. Invasion of Tbilisi, guerrilla and urban warfare seemed inevitable. Russian troops also pushed into Western Georgia's Samegrelo and Guria regions from the territory of Abkhazia which had been under Russia's de facto occupation since the 1990s. This temporarily paralyzed work of Georgia's Black Sea port.

At some point during the invasion, I briefly left my ministry to see the family and return back. It was close to midnight. Traffic was light and I drove fast. Georgia of 2008 was different from what it was before the Revolution of Roses. Infrastructure was upgraded, public safety improved and public institutions modernized. Traffic rules were observed and streets were safe. It felt like driving through a peaceful and modern European city awash in street lights. I switched on radio. Main local stations were broadcasting the sound of ringing bells. People were hearing the same sound during medieval incursions.

In August of 2008, President of Georgia was 40 years old, Prime Minister 37 years old, Minister of Defense 30 years old, Minister of Interior 40 years old, Minister of Foreign Affairs 31 years old and Minister of Finance 33 years old.

Resilience of Georgia's political leadership, resistance by the army and mediation by the European Union and the United States helped to halt Russia's advance to Tbilisi. Georgia's image as the top reformer helped. An agreement brokered by the French president helped to stop the war but it was ad hoc and did not propose a conflict resolution. Despite risks to personal safety, presidents of Estonia, Latvia, Lithuania, Poland and Ukraine flew to Georgia to take part in an anti-occupation nighttime rally in Tbilisi on 12 August and to serve as the human shield. Later in August, Russia recognized independence of Abkhazia and of South Ossetia. Recognition by Venezuela, Nicaragua and Nauru followed.

The war of 2008 was among opening salvos in Russia's effort to reimpose suzerainty over the former Soviet space. Russia's invasion of Ukraine from 2014, Russia's December 2021 demand to rescind the 2008 NATO Bucharest summit decision by banning Ukraine and Georgia from entering NATO and Russia's all-out assault against Ukraine from 2022 transformed global politics and reduced Europe's "wind of change" of the 1990s to a whisper in earphones.

A number of foreign politicians, international bureaucrats and pundits who in a rush of a self-serving and an ultimately self-defeating thinking discarded the 2008 war as the one-off incident or worked to split the blame between Georgia and Russia should acknowledge their blunder... and revise their memoirs.

This adverse geopolitics affects Georgia politically and economically. It impacts the national governance. Abkhazia, with its breathtaking coastline and a famous tourism franchise, has become a shadow of its own self demographically and economically. Samachablo became an impasse housing Russian troops. Some 80% of Georgians support membership in the European Union and in NATO...[2]

Georgia's situation raises—for me at least—three questions:

[2] Public Opinion Survey, Residents of Georgia (September–October 2019), *Center for Insights in Survey Research*, a Project of the International Republican Institute.

1. How can an open society resist a much larger hostile foreign power which exploits such openness to push back against a democratic modernization in a region where a lasting peace and development cannot be taken for granted?
2. How far can a domestic centralization of power stretch when hybrid anti-Western external and internal threats to the national security must be contained so that the statehood is not undone with the next election?
3. This book explains Georgia in the bipolar world (Soviet years) and in the West-dominated world. What are the national security and national governance implications of a geoeconomic and geopolitical multipolarity in which big powers fight for influence?

CHAPTER 6

Public Leadership

Abstract This chapter discusses three main qualities of a public leader—vision, courage and altruism. All three are equally important—a leader lacking even one quality is at best inefficient and at worst dangerous. The chapter explains what it takes to disrupt *and* reengineer in the wake of significant electoral changes and street-led revolutions. It is based on the author's personal meetings with and observation of public leaders in different countries.

Keywords Leadership · Vision · Courage · Altruism

Triangle is the strongest, inherently rigid geometric shape. Apply pressure to a triangle made of rods connected to each other with flexible hinges and it will not deform. Similarly, a three-legged stool is inherently stable—it will not wobble even on an uneven surface.

Likewise, successful leaders (especially in developing countries with immature institutions) must display three qualities: *vision, courage and altruism*. Without this, their countries are "black holes." You can throw at them international assistance, but a real transformation does not happen.

Without *vision*, leaders are path-dependent. They cannot think outside of the box and cannot discover niches where their countries can prosper. Mentally and behaviorally, they are weather wanes more than signposts.

D. Gvindadze, *The Transformation of Georgia from 2004 to 2012*,
https://doi.org/10.1007/978-3-031-18264-8_6

With no grand designs, they think tactically rather than strategically. They are overwhelmed by the routine, unable to predict main threats to national security and act wisely before these threats materialize. Instead of setting ambitious targets and then reverse engineering to devise strategies to achieve them, they boast of isolated reforms. They swim along the shore, scared of deeper waters which might be more treacherous but more promising. They fail to act on new technological and geoeconomic trends. They eschew esoteric ideas which voters might perceive as detached from their routines. They make no daring moves in spatial and urban planning, institutional modernization, law and order, innovation and technology. They appease rather than resolve. They are cautious and transactional, preoccupied by own exit strategies. They rely too much on a zigzagging international discourse on economic development theories. They cannot execute an overarching design wedding together multiple schools of thought—liberalism, libertarianism, interventionism, socialism, etc.[1]

Visionary leaders understand that even an insignificant misstep at their level may tear things apart at lower levels, unleashing social, political and geopolitical tremors with higher-order effects and life cycles of their own. They understand historical, ethnic, social, emotional and other features of societies they lead and engage these societies in a way which is rational, idealistic and ambitious. Visionary leaders have a predictive national security mindset—they act early on emerging threats. They seek to create legacies that last across multiple electoral cycles. They know when to exit politics.

Vision is about understanding the soul of a nation, about maintaining a personal style which broadens the margin of manoeuver when choices and trade-offs are painful. Visionary leaders build resilient social contracts. In developing countries, they not only preside over their nations but rebuild and reengineer those nations. They produce ideologies which inform all other choices. They also know that ideologies perish if the leadership is missing. Visionary leaders understand how intimidating the power of a public servant might be and how important it is that such power is

[1] In his book From Third World to First. The Singapore Story: 1965–2000, Singapore's founding father Lee Kuan Yew brings examples where his vision and his deeds defied conventional wisdom and were misunderstood by many inside Singapore and internationally.

properly harnessed and restrained. Visionaries might be perceived unreasonable by those who prioritize political correctness and certainty over substance, or impulsive by external observers better steeped in tutoring than in listening and learning.

Vision allows to talk on par with leaders of more powerful nations. The latter discern whether their interlocutor from a smaller country is free from inferiority complexes. Vision of a leader draws in a talent. It minimizes nihilism among civil servants who to the question *"how are you in the new job?"* do not answer "*I will give it a try, they are trying to do something [note: "they" refers to a government the civil servant works in; it ought to be "we" and not "they"]; I will not stay long, my past employer pledged to accept me back"* or *"do not congratulate me on my new job, it is more like condolences."* I have heard these two answers time and again in countries with a slim chance of a breakthrough.

Without *courage*, leaders cannot disrupt a status quo. They are suspicious of innovation and scared that the future will cannibalize the present. They may set a goal but fail to implement it because they cannot manage operational risks. Instead, they settle for an accommodation which, behind smokescreens, perpetuates an economic, political and mental slack. They avoid revolutionary tactics, even if the latter offers the only escape route out of poverty. They are more at ease with a "bottom-up" discourse where grassroots pressures and low-octane technocratic efforts are supposed to result in incremental changes.

Leaders without courage like euphemisms. Addressing corruption, they say *"it is time for holistic measures which would prepare ground for reduction of corruption opportunities, and for this we need a new legislation and new anti-corruption councils and agencies."* But they are reluctant to single out "patient zero" and act upon the understanding that anything short of confronting the "patient zero" means fighting a symptom and not a root cause of a problem. They never say "*Mr. X stole amount Y from a company Z and so Mr. X must be punished now."*

Without public leaders acting as bulldozers and minesweepers, inhabitants of lower decks of governments hedge their bets. They do not confront transnational crime with geopolitical undertones. They do not oppose clans which monopolize strategic sectors, fund parliamentary factions, payroll ministers, plunder state-owned enterprises and banks. They dodge individual responsibility, scared to put themselves in harm's way. This lowers the odds of hitting a home run for their countries.

Any election or a street-led revolution raises expectations of improved living conditions. An electoral or a post-revolutionary breakthrough entails disruption which makes enemies and friends. Enemies may represent a more consolidated class which obstructs, shames, blames and blackmails. How should a leader respond? Waste months to drum up consensus around *all* issues to dilute personal responsibility, knowing that a post-electoral honeymoon cannot last? Or, take a *personal* risk to get things done fast, to be consequential more than congenial? Courage is never collective. It is manifestly individual, especially in countries where institutions are weak and allegiance of law enforcers changes with political cycles.

Courageous leaders blaze unique trails for their nations and create for themselves powerful enemies even when they know that they might one day face those enemies without bodyguards or armored vehicles, and maybe in exiles. Courageous leaders prosecute misbehavior in own ranks, even when a punishment must be administered to contributors to their own ascent to power.

Altruism is the precondition for a long-term legitimacy. Imagine a leader who allows his inner circle to abuse his public office to grow a business. Or a leader who, devising infrastructural or investment plans, thinks how to profit personally. Such multitasking destroys legitimacy. Illegitimate leaders are less likely to rally their nations around a flag.

To sum it up: vision, courage and altruism are equally important. Having two qualities out of three is insufficient. For example, kleptocrats may be courageous and have a vision. Without courage, they cannot succeed in their own way, while vision helps them to stay afloat in toxic environments. However, without the third quality—altruism—the first two qualities are futile. They may make leaders more dangerous than if they lacked courage or vision.

Remove one rod from a triangle or a leg from a three-legged stool and you lose a geometric shape and a support structure. The remaining two rods start moving pointlessly against each other and a two-legged stool collapses.

CHAPTER 7

The Ten Commandments of State Building

Abstract This chapter explains ten pillars of a successful state building: leadership, national memory and objectives, sense of urgency, risk-taking, political consolidation, law and order, national security, public institutions and services, integrity and communication. Without most of these ten pillars, even best technocrats fail. Or, they soldier on as unimportant preachers.

Keywords State building · Leadership · National memory · Urgency · Independent thinking · Risk-taking · Political consolidation · Law and order · National security · Public institutions and services · Integrity · Communication

Imagine reforms-minded well-educated technocrats in ministries of finance and economy or in central banks of developing countries. Imagine them lacking a political backing. Can they reform state-owned enterprises captured by powerful clans? Can they restrain pork barrel spending? Can they reform or abolish public entities and programs which add no value but employ voters? Can they protect their financial sectors from raiders and money launderers? Can they prevent public subsidies, directed lending or guarantees which trigger liabilities for future generations without creating public value? Can they hold the line against increasing

D. Gvindadze, *The Transformation of Georgia from 2004 to 2012*,
https://doi.org/10.1007/978-3-031-18264-8_7

salaries and pensions beyond what their economies can sustain? Can they instill a new spirit into a public administration? Can they confront threats from a "strategic" corruption?[1] Can they act fast, without endless consultations to dilute individual risks and responsibilities? Can they provide credible assurances to investors?

The answer is *no*. To succeed individually *and* collectively, reformers must operate in a conducive ecosystem. What follows is an overview of key pillars of such ecosystem with links to Georgia's experience.

1. **Leadership**. Public institutions restrain "animal spirits," prescribe bandwidths of action and establish safety valves for emotional and political outbursts. But they cannot replace leadership. In developing countries with immature institutions, assertions to the contrary do not hold empirically.

   Georgia's public leadership of 2004-2012 reverberated across all layers of the government, encouraging and enforcing the sense of purpose and of direction in the realm of domestic and foreign policies. It aimed at parting ways with defeatism and apathies of Georgia's recent past. This mode of leadership—visionary, courageous, altruist, forceful, omnipresent and at times overbearing or maximalist—was not immune to mistakes. But it served to promote Georgia's national interest and Georgia's international appeal. In 2004-2012, Georgia went through a grand disruption and a grand reengineering. The Revolution of Roses changed Georgia for the better. Its ultimate legacy will crystallize with passage of time across multiple electoral cycles.

2. **National memory and objectives**. Past influences the future. It is impossible to design the right future without a comprehensive understanding of the past. A strong national memory—a historic narrative to which most of a nation subscribes—helps to foretell

[1] Strategic corruption refers to effort by some countries "to take the kind of corruption that was previously a mere feature of their own political systems and transform it into a weapon on the global stage" and "into an instrument of national strategy." P. Zelikow, E.Edelman, K. Harrison, C. Ward Gventer (July/August 2020). The Rise of Strategic Corruption, How States Weaponise Graft. *Foreign Affairs*.

future risks and to set national objectives. Nations which misread their past misconstrue their future.

Georgia's objective in 2004-2012—based on analysis of its past, of the regional context and on the international window of opportunity—was, *inter alia*, the European and the Euroatlantic integration and the transformation into a regional hub for investment, manufacturing, services, logistics and trade.

3. **Sense of urgency and independent thinking**. Georgia's 2003 GDP per capita was approximately US$ 1000, much less than in the European Union. Poland's GDP per capita in 2003 was US$ 5,700. To reach Poland's GDP per capita of 2003, Georgia's GDP per capita would have to grow annually by 20% in nominal US$ terms for ten years.[2] Such growth offered the only path to the economic convergence and it required bold measures.

   Key positions in Georgia's government of 2004-2012 were held by "small government fundamentalists" who led the economic liberalization. This did not preclude a "big push" from the state in the context of spatial planning and infrastructural development. Libertarians, liberals, institutionalists, interventionists, fiscal hawks—it was a mix of individuals united around one overarching vision. Government interventionism did not mean a premature welfare state. In sum, Georgia's development model was composite. In 2014-2012, a handful of experts questioned whether Georgia's EU path was consistent with the "Singapore model" that they thought Georgia was pursuing. They were biased or ignorant.

4. **Risk-taking.** Stakeholder engagement fosters consensus around decisions involving multiple constituencies and mitigates risks of

[2] Growth of GDP per capita in nominal US$ terms does not fully reflect real GDP growth (growth in volume of economic output) and growth of purchasing power of a population, although it does capture growth in volume and value of economic output, price and exchange rate dynamics. Furthermore, countries are ranked into low-, middle- and high-income categories mainly based on the nominal GDP per capita in current US$ terms; hence, the given metrics provide a basis for cross-country comparison of levels of economic development.

reversals. But any engagement must end timely with a judgment call, even if a buy-in is not universal. Trade-offs between the speed, efficiency and inclusiveness of the decision-making are country-specific. Georgia of 2004–2012 owes its success to people taking individual risks fighting crime and corruption and building modern institutions.

5. **Political consolidation**. In the presidential elections of 15 January 2004—the first elections after the Revolution of Roses—Mikheil Saakashvili received 96.27% of votes. In the parliamentary elections of 28 March 2004, the United National Movement (UNM) led by the president obtained 66.24% of votes. The UNM obtained a landslide victory in local elections of 2006. By the end of the first presidential term, ratings decreased, although remained at a high level. In presidential elections of 2008, President Saakashvili obtained 53.41% of votes—almost twice higher than votes for his main contender (although the contender won in Tbilisi by garnering 40.43% of votes, almost 8% higher than the president). In parliamentary elections of 2008, the UNM obtained 53.45% of votes, almost twice higher than a second-best contender. In local elections of 2010, the UNM again won comfortably in Tbilisi and regions. Until the parliamentary elections of October 2012 when the UNM lost to the Georgian Dream coalition, the UNM controlled both the executive and the legislature. This enhanced efficiency and minimized political horse-trading, although the concentration of power in Georgia's institutionally immature setting might have amplified opportunities for missteps.

   Even when a political class is ostensibly consolidated, public officials retain their egos and allegiances. They compete, miscalculate, surprise on the upside and frustrate. Individual mistakes—even minor mistakes related to a personal style—hit entire teams. Governments are complex, but voters perceive them as uniform creations bearing collective responsibilities.

6. **Law and order.** People worrying about personal safety do not spend or invest. They hide assets and income from tax declarations. They live below a threshold of attention of criminals and officials.

Their defensiveness harms entrepreneurship. When breach of public safety results in tragedies, people siphon their money abroad and leave.

In the 2000s-2010s, Georgian criminal bosses ("thieves-in-law") represented almost a third of the criminal underworld leaders in Moscow and more than a half across Russia.[3] Before the 2003 Revolution of Roses, they maintained strong influence in Georgia where romanticization of a criminal culture was not uncommon. From the Soviet days, criminals had been used for political purposes. Some became part of Russia's toolbox of a geopolitical influence.

Zero tolerance to crime from 2004 drove criminals out of Georgia and helped to establish credibility early on. The anti-corruption campaign entailed punishments within own ranks, closure of fraudulent schemes and exposure of powerful individuals. Prosecution targeted both petty and elite corruption. Criminal underworld membership became criminalized. Criminals' influence on streets, businesses and politics vanished. This enabled reformers to take on vested interests. Police, the most despised public institution, was restaffed and rebranded. In mid-2012, 88% of Georgia's residents described their confidence in the police as favorable. Patrol police, where almost the entire police force was fired and new officers were hired and trained, rose to one of the highest approval ratings among public institutions. New police offices had glass walls to signal that police is not scared of criminals and of transparency.

Global media soon ranked Georgia among the safest destinations for tourism and leisure. Remote locations—mountains, natural reserves—not recommended for visiting in the 1990s became safe for domestic and foreign travelers. In a 2012 survey, Georgians declared reduced crime as the most important achievement of the government. Public safety was no longer among issues which households were facing.[4]

Prosecution of crime and corruption increased prison population from approximately 7,000 in 2003 to 20,000 in 2012. In per capita

[3] M. Galeotti (2018).

[4] Georgian National Study (June-July 2012), International Republican Institute (http://www.iri.org/sites/default/files/2012%20August%2020%20Survey%20Georgian%20Public%20Opinion%2C%20June%2026-July%204%2C%202012.pdf retrieved on 4 April 2017).

terms, this was in the top-ten of the prison population rates globally.[5] The administration of justice was modernized and purged of corruption, but in 2004-2012 it was not fully independent as Georgia's national security risks and the desire to progress fast pushed the authorities toward tightening controls and strengthening defenses.

7. **National security**. In 2004–2012, defense, intelligence, counterintelligence, countercrime and counterterrorism professionals were certain that their country was behind them.

   Any doubt about adherence to this principle across multiple electoral cycles can cause failures undoing decades of progress. Dangers follow defenders of the national interest and their families long after they end their careers. Inability of a state—and in the most shameful of circumstances an unwillingness of the state—to protect these people destroys credibility. If floodgates of the national security are breached, economic reforms become futile. A state—however well reformed and skillfully spinned—becomes porous and may unravel. It then takes years of bravery and brinkmanship to rebuild those floodgates.

8. **Public institutions and services.** Institutional transformation in Georgia entered a new phase from 2004. It started with downsizing and restructuring and continued with granular work to modernize and rebrand institutions and services. Agencies interacting with citizens—public and civil registries, tax and customs, service centers of the Ministry of Interior, front offices in municipalities and ministries—were restaffed and modernized. Suspicious characters handling paper-based tasks and taking bribes in smoky closed-door Soviet-era offices along dim corridors were replaced with young professionals handling computer-based tasks in modern open spaces and following clear protocols and deadlines. By 2012, Georgia's public services were the most advanced in the region. This reduced corruption at the point of delivery of public services.

[5] The World Prison Brief database https://www.prisonstudies.org/ (retrieved on 11 October 2019).

Public services developed in 2004-2012 largely survived the political change in 2012. But institutions of the law enforcement and the administration of justice did not develop sufficient immunity to politics. A lower politicization of these institutions might have alleviated post-electoral dramas and retributions from 2012. Whether full institutional depoliticization in 2004-2012 was feasible is an open question.

9. **Integrity.** Staying beyond reproach—individually and as a government—helps to keep faith with people and broadens margin of manoeuver. Personal integrity and integrity of inner circles enhance resilience.

   Georgia's success in 2004-2012 owes to the government's focus on a public interest and not on a personal gain. A vast majority of civil servants who exited the government in 2012 started lives from scratch with meager savings. Revolving doors which normally allow exiting public officials to work in the private sector malfunctioned in Georgia's polarized environment.

10. **Communication.** Reforms can be misunderstood and misrepresented. Populists can confuse voters lacking understanding of how decisions, choices and constraints influence the state building. Part of any society trusts conspiracy theories. Strategic communication generates space for reforms and positive spin is important. At times, it may transcend substance, but it cannot outdo it.

    Georgia depends on the international good will, so in 2004-2012 a significant effort was invested into explaining—domestically and internationally—Georgia's state building and how it reflected threats, constraints and opportunities. Such explanation was partially successful.

Without most of these ten pillars in place, even good technocrats soldier on as unimportant preachers. Long strategies, roadmaps, brainstorming rounds and foreign experts cannot help.

Lack of the state building does not mean that developing countries do not undertake macroeconomic adjustments. They do, to the international ovation, because forces fueling, say, a devaluation of national currencies are too tectonic to be resisted by vested interests. Even in places where vested interests control large swaths of economies they acquiesce to external and internal macroeconomic adjustments which hit their net worth in hard currency terms. But macroeconomic adjustments bring stabilization, not growth. To spur a post-adjustment growth, countries must reform their state-owned enterprises and banks, prosecute state capture, crime and mismanagement. This is where—in the absence of a resolute state building—a full armor of political, criminal, financial and geopolitical connections springs into action to obstruct reforms which bite individually despite helping nationally. Unless confronted head-on, enemies of a strong statehood continue their business as usual.

CHAPTER 8

National Governance

Abstract This chapter explains risks that might be faced by countries when their state building halts, to futility of isolated reforms in a bad national governance context and to complexities of shifting from bad to good national governance.

Keywords Clan · State capture · Autocrat · Kleptocrat · Oligarch

Which national governance best promotes a sustained economic growth, protects fundamental rights and freedoms and unlocks people's potential? What are people-level implications of a bad national governance? Is there a path back from a bad to good national governance? Can an isolated reform be a game changer when the national governance fails? The answer is no, as explained in this chapter.

The narrative that follows is intentionally abstract (different forms of national governance trigger different outcomes in countries with different internal and external circumstances; successful off-the-shelf solutions are rare), but it explains likely challenges in places ruled by autocrats, kleptocrats and oligarchs (in this chapter, "clans," "clansmen").

In larger countries, ruling clans and their industrial-media-political-banking empires might evolve into hills surrounded by moats. Ordinary businessmen grow to a certain size and operate in green pastures in

D. Gvindadze, *The Transformation of Georgia from 2004 to 2012*,
https://doi.org/10.1007/978-3-031-18264-8_8

between these hills. An under-soil of such societies is corroded and level playing fields do not exist. What ensues is a social, emotional and economic quagmire where the clans shape electoral outcomes, clash, compete or co-exist. Such countries may resemble a managed multipolar anarchy or a more orderly and centralized formation. Much depends on a national leader, although a control the latter exercises cannot be full. Key decisions are taken below public radars. Competition among clans might balance off their influences and help to conduct elections which at first glance are not stolen. The "not stolen" is the overstatement because electoral outcomes are not decided only on the election day.

A small country might evolve into a monogarchy where one or interconnected clans seize even the mentioned green pastures. Instead of the hills and moats, they erect countrywide mountains, residing on top of them and coercing others to head for exits or to subsist on slopes. State monopolizes corruption. When countries fight for their economic or geopolitical survival, corruption is not a trivial offense. It is the state treason with no statute of limitation. Risks to orderly political successions grow. Each election is a crisis for individuals, businesses and foreign partners. Long-term planning suffers. Pathways of success become narrow, dependent on leaders' health and on their ability to score wins.

Top seats in such countries provide an unfettered access to public finances. They allow to exploit state-owned enterprises and banks, to manipulate through abuse of a modern surveillance state, control of the judiciary and prosecution. Public procurement becomes part of the power consolidation effort: cronies and political donors secure lucrative contracts. Natural resources and economic assets end up in clans' ownership. Politicization of real sectors over-exposes banks to politically vulnerable clients. Composition of private investment changes: not all are ready to compete on a slope against a strong rival attacking from above. Quality investors exit. Insiders gain share. They rule, legislate and invest at the same time. Foreign investors unwilling to cozy up with local elites stay away because having a local business partner who is too powerful politically means that he can raid you. Clans view unrelated rich people with social and political capital as a threat because the latter may support opposition. They try to co-opt them (in which case such rich people end up in fragile and uneven alliances) or to destroy them reputationally and financially. Public institutions are forced into direct and contingent liabilities and cost-sharing arrangements which benefit a few at the expense of many. Independent media and a real opposition are defunded and persecuted. A ruler monopolizes charity work in pursuance of own political goals. Politics, money, crime and geopolitics merge, inhibiting electoral freedom and fairness. Multiplication of fake opposition parties dilutes the real opposition, saws confusion and impairs quality of a public debate. Privileged bequeath privilege to their kids. Societies become hereditary. Social stratification strengthens, social mobility ends and social cohesion weakens. A positive correlation between experience and education of public servants and their performance breaks. An imitation of a democratic governance ensues. Such countries might become geopolitically porous and vulnerable to a transnational crime. International calls for a good governance fall on deaf ears.

The noose around the democracy tightens not through a "rule of law," but through a "rule by law" where the spirit of the law is neglected whereas the pursuit of the letter of the law is ruthless and indiscriminate. Not all can contextualize this direction of travel until it is too late. Even when the direction is understood, its many elements might seem individually immaterial to act on. For example, elite corruption (manipulation of prices of fuel, gas and electricity, privatization) is more sophisticated and less visible than bribery at the point of delivery of public services. Not all voters can comprehend and act upon it.

Large businessmen might be tempted to strike "gentleman" deals with ruling clans, hoping that these would hold. The hopes end in tears—the rulers impose their will through prosecution, tax and customs administrations, inspection agencies and courts that they control. They dusts off old cases and fabricate false charges. Clapping to ruminations of a ruler speaking at an assembly of business leaders thus buys only a weak conditional immunity. Developing countries' immature laws and procedures often lead to ad hoc decision-making. Almost anyone who exercised responsibility in public or private sectors can be prosecuted for minor deviations. A statute of limitations is ignored.

Independent journalists and the real opposition face asphyxiating pressures. Some change careers to feed families. Others resist, braving harassment by law enforcement units and blackmail through video footages. They hold on despite mental strains to which they confess to closest inner circles. Their personal lives suffer. Such people deserve praise. Dedication of best years to improving the national governance—and to serving sentences as political prisoners—is an act of valor.

Public officials taking on clans are resistance fighters. Think of cutting influential middlemen in an energy sector, of downsizing a lucrative bureaucracy, of arbitrating disputes involving powerful players or of ending fraud in a banking sector. These tasks are dangerous. Reprisals can materialize after an end of public tenures. Such public officials deserve safeguards (job, political protection) provided, *inter alia*, by the international community. Because when in office they are the best hope of the international community.

A break-down of the resistance strengthens the asphyxiation further. Independent courts and free media are eviscerated. Defencelessness creeps in. Human rights, including property rights, are smashed. Lawlessness grows in places with traditions of romanticization of a criminal underculture. Investigative journalists become braver than law enforcers. Middle class disappears. Surveillance technologies transform countries into disciplinary panopticons where good public servants whisper fearing eavesdropping in their offices, where people are filmed in their apartments through cameras in TV sets and drones hovering at their windows, where a contact with someone holding different views invites wrath of law enforcers, where people switch off mobiles in cafes, where a restaurant reservation should not be made from a personal phone because a reserved table might get immediately equipped with a microphone.

Jobs disappear. Local offices of international organizations and foreign embassies end up offering the best jobs. Emigration gains pace. Seasonal workers and youth leave and never return. Countries "grow old before they get rich." Increase in old-age dependency ratios (the number of pensioners as a share of working-age people) strains public budgets and inhibits spending on education and infrastructure because budgets are earmarked to social protection. The impact on emigration of these "push factors" is compounded by "pull factors"—for example, when people are attracted by better job and social safety prospects in advanced economies. Growth stalls and national debt piles up. Odds of a youthful and entrepreneurial society diminish. Poor are more vulnerable to political manipulations and to conspiracy theories. Poverty and emigration divert attention away from the elite corruption. Individuals in daily survival mode are docile and uncertain about their ability to exert influence. They do not see a direct link between their votes and electoral outcomes. Electoral perks—a bag of fruits and vegetables, a promise to retain eligibility for a social assistance, a prospect of a blue collar job—trump anything else. This fight for survival at lower decks is not correlated with opulence in a captain's (ruler's) cabin. A ruler's priority is to strengthen floodgates between lower decks and luxury suites and to ensure that a discontent at lower decks stays below a boiling point. The floodgates in this case are loyal police squads, a kompromat and a prosecution.

I think of one town which I first visited in the early 2000s. Streets, restaurants, cafes and night clubs were packed. Traffic jams were not uncommon. Youth crowded entries to schools and universities. The city was not rich, but it was cheerful. I visited the same place a decade later. Walking in the downtown, past familiar thoroughfares and parks, the sense of loneliness was overpowering. Cracked trottoirs, worn down roads, dry fountains, half-empty municipal parks and commercial spaces, stray dogs. Many people had emigrated. Even if the national governance improves, only a slim portion might return. Had the rubicon been passed?

In countries where institutional guardrails exist and electoral democracy works, politicians' behavior oscillates within a bandwidth. "Captured" countries have no such guardrails. Because power is used mainly for personal enrichment, elections create financial and personal safety risks. Blocking political successions, rulers end up on slippery slopes. Their popularity decreases, so they become more authoritarian to retain power. Each political term is more oppressive and more Orwellian. Autocrats deal with autocrats; this influences structure of their international partnerships.

Political breakthroughs in such countries—electoral and revolutionary—are usually abrupt and confrontational. In the best case, an old guard is swept away and capable new protest leaders play on a greenfield. More likely, by coopting or destroying main protest leaders and infiltrating opposition parties, clans behind a state capture permanently impair a statehood, weakening a correlation between electoral outcomes, voter support and a real influence. An ensuing semblance of stability prevents positive breakthroughs.

Revolutions attract opportunists. Revolutions succeed if opportunists are exfiltrated and idealists are mainstreamed. A path from a revolution to development is not automatic. Procrastination reduces prospects of a breakthrough. Modern clans embrace virtues of legality and of sophistication. Their money, transnational networks and media ownership bring influence over politicians. Their lawyers, accountants and managers erect safeguards against reversals of their fortune through foreign litigation and arbitration clauses.

If a national ambition is convergence with high-income countries, bargains with clans are Faustian. Except in very rare cases where clans are directed by their home country authorities to serve geopolitical objectives (think, for example, of certain wealthy Russians who wanted to move on but ended up in an eternal service of the state where they amassed wealth, facing the "just as I thought I was out they pull me back in" dilemmas), recruitment of clans into the service of a state creates risks of a reverse recruitment. This weakens national immunity to the "strategic corruption" threats from foreign adversaries which weaponize corruption as an instrument of their geopolitical strategies.[1]

End of the state capture requires strong leaders. Public institutions cannot lead as they are penetrated. International best practice does not exist. Held together by a "collective criminal liability," clans resist. Through their media and lobbyists, they protest an "assault on good governance and democracy," the very ideals that state builders seek to enforce. In this fight, consolidation of power helps. An interpretation of events depends on wisdom of local and foreign opinion-makers.

Expropriation of illegal assets is an upright promise. But an abrupt countrywide redesign of an entrenched structure of ownership can halt investment and trigger capital destruction. Most of such assets might have been appropriated decades ago. Lawyers and accountants make these contracts difficult to unwind. An alternative to the unwinding of established contracts is an enforcement of new rules and improvement of a business climate to foster new market entries and dilute clans' influence. Investment into modern sectors of economy diminishes dependence on traditional industries. Clans thus lose privileges and become ordinary businesspeople. Precondition—credibility of the new rules and a real buy-in from clans. If the latter does not exist, state builders must up the ante considerably.

A one-off success (a vibrant state building spanning a limited number of electoral cycles, for example) does not automatically entail a positive legacy. The odds of a complete remission (where the cancer of a bad national governance ends) are lower than the odds of a temporary remission (where a short-term relief does not mean that the cancer is defeated). We lack a strong cross-country evidence of the remission enduring beyond one or two electoral cycles. Because cancer treatment is difficult, focus must be on prevention.

For the West and international organizations, captured countries are mine fields where standard tools malfunction. A polite advocacy has a

[1] A footnote in Chapter 7 defines strategic corruption.

marginal impact. Seeking to stop a political deterioration in such countries, these foreign players face a riposte: we enforce laws—don't you agree that laws must be enforced? Only the best statesmen, diplomats and international civil servants comprehend the big picture, its cultural, social, historical and geopolitical genesis. Only the boldest confront problems properly despite information asymmetries. Only the wisest act on early emerging trends to contain a snowball before it becomes an avalanche.

CHAPTER 9

Size and Effectiveness of a Government

Abstract This chapter explains the relationship between economic growth, size and effectiveness of a government. It shows evolution of Georgia's government expenditure in 2004–2012. Key messages: (1) big government does not mean high growth; (2) where government size is unrestricted legally or through a time-tested political consensus, it is likely to increase across electoral cycles; (3) effective governments can create more value than inert oversize bureaucracies and (4) thinking in terms of an opportunity cost is key to an efficient budget planning and execution.

Keywords Government size · Government effectiveness · Liberty Act · Opportunity cost

Investors, consumers, lenders and depositors depend on soundness of countries' sovereign balance sheets. Sovereign risks feed into investee firms' risk profiles and influence "hurdle rates"—minimum rates of return on investments sought from such firms. High hurdle rates upset investability of projects, reducing investment and consumption. Country ceilings—rating assigned to sovereigns by international credit rating agencies (including Standard and Poor's, Fitch and Moody's)—often set upper constraints on credit ratings for local banks and firms and influence cost of funds and a flow of credit.

D. Gvindadze, *The Transformation of Georgia from 2004 to 2012*,
https://doi.org/10.1007/978-3-031-18264-8_9

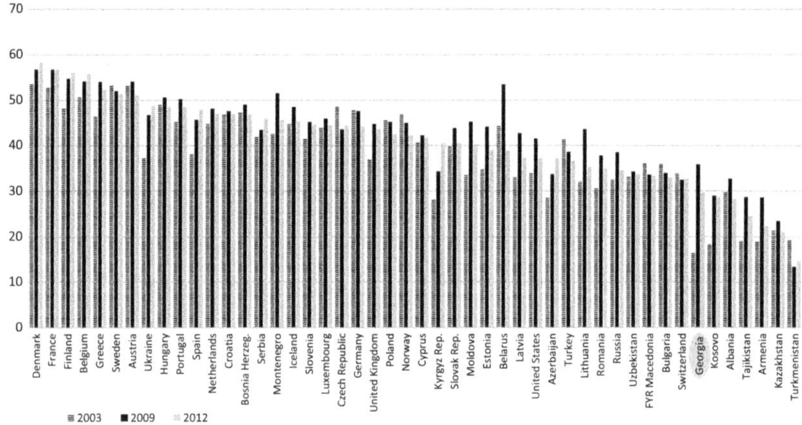

Fig. 9.1 Total general government expenditure as percent of GDP in 2003, 2009 and 2012 (ranked by 2012 ratios, largest to smallest) (*Source* International Monetary Fund. World Economic Outlook and country reports)

Views on size and a raison d'être of governments influence national development paths. Government expenditure to GDP ratios differs across countries and evolves over time. In 2004–2012, this ratio increased in many countries, partly due to a fiscal stimulus to mitigate the impact of the global economic downturn from 2008 to 2009. The ratio was mainly higher in advanced economies (Fig. 9.1).

At 16.5% in 2003, Georgia's ratio of total general government expenditure to GDP was the lowest among countries in Fig. 9.1. It increased to 35.8% in 2009 due to the post-2008/2009 fiscal stimulus and then decreased to 29.6% in 2012 (seventh lowest ratio in the Fig. 9.1).

One key factor which allowed to increase government expenditure without excessive fiscal imbalances was Georgia's tax reform from 2004 discussed in Chapter 14. Tax and customs revenues as percent of GDP increased from 14% in 2003 to almost 26% in 2007 in the context of much lower tax rates and of drastically reduced number of taxes. This stimulated investment into the national security, infrastructure, social services, public institutions and services.

In 2011, to restrict the government size, Georgia's Parliament adopted the Liberty Act—an organic law on economic freedom which limited the general government expenditure to 30% of GDP and the overall budget deficit to 3% of GDP. According to the Act, if a budget law which the Parliament adopts for a coming fiscal year breaches these two limits, the government must implement a plan of return to full compliance with the limits within two years. The Parliament allows such deviation only if in the current fiscal year the limits are observed. Georgia thus asserted its vision of limits of the government while retaining the agility to handle ad hoc events.

The thinking behind the Liberty Act was as follows:

- **Politics plays out in the short term and might neglect longer-term consequences.** Where a government size is unrestricted legally or through a time-tested multistakeholder political consensus, it is likely to increase under the weight of bureaucracy and of electoral cycles. Hence, limit the government and seek private sector solutions or public–private partnerships to divert pressure from budget (Chapter 11 explains a market-based approach in agriculture and healthcare).
- **A big government does not mean high growth.** Figure 9.2 plots growth against the size of governments (global dataset, certain outliers removed). The weak inverse relationship holds even when countries are categorized by their GDP per capita to compare countries in similar economic circumstances. At certain medium- to low-income levels, the relationship at times becomes positive, although the trend is not pronounced.
- **Effective governments create more value than inert oversize bureaucracies.** In 2004–2012, Georgia's improvement in the Government Effectiveness Indicator (1.09 point improvement, from − 0.49 in 2004 to + 0.6 in 2012) was the highest *globally*. At its level of GDP per capita, Georgia's 2012 government effectiveness indicator (+0.6) was the highest *globally*.[1]
- **Not all public servants think of government spending in terms of an opportunity cost.** Officials without a private sector background might misunderstand the wealth creation process. Or, they

[1] Government Effectiveness captures perceptions of the quality of public services, the quality of the civil service and the degree of its independence from political pressures, the quality of policy formulation and implementation, and the credibility of the government's commitment to such policies. Source: Worldwide Governance indicators http://info.worldbank.org/governance/wgi/

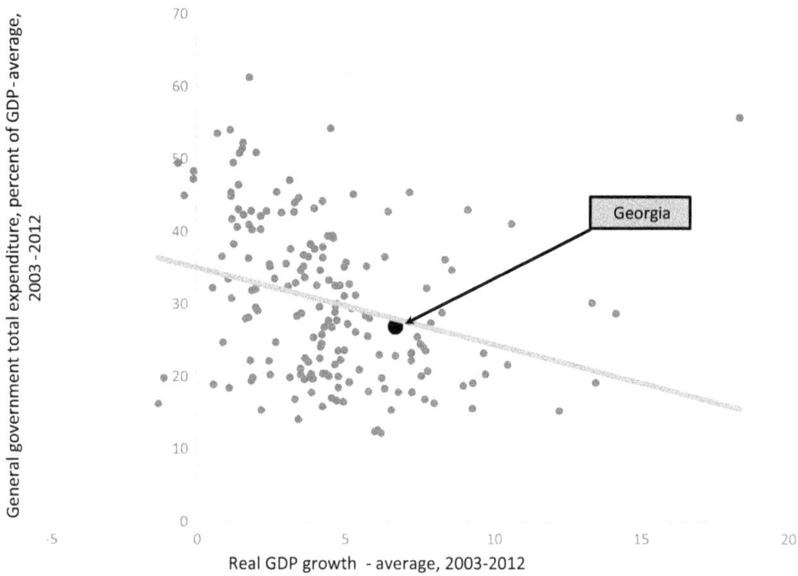

Fig. 9.2 Government size and real GDP growth (average for 2003–2012, all countries) (*Source* International Monetary Fund. World Economic Outlook)

understand in theory without having created wealth and paid taxes as entrepreneurs. This blurs judgment on what to fund from a budget and what not. Profligate spending ensues. Imagine a minister who is proposed to earmark US$ 10 million to construct a new office building. Would he/she agree? Under which circumstances? Does he/she grasp the order of magnitude of the proposal? How many entrepreneurs would have to work to generate the US$ 10 million in taxes?

CHAPTER 10

Structure of a Public Expenditure

Abstract This chapter discusses an optimum structure of public expenditure. It provides a cross-country comparison of infrastructure spending and explains how infrastructure projects in Georgia crowded in private investors and multiplied the impact of the budget spending. It explains public–private partnerships—their benefits and risks.

Keywords Capital and recurrent spending · Budget deficit · Public–private partnership

National budgets mirror evolving social contracts between political leaders and citizens, stages of political, cultural, emotional and economic development, attitudes to virtues and limits of public action. Fractured and polarized politics leads to complex trade-offs and compromises. Political polarization and fragmentation in developing countries make holding the line on a proper composition of government expenditure difficult. It may increase wasteful subsidies, unsustainable social outlays and premature inflation indexation mechanisms. This creates an illusion of welfare societies even when per capita incomes are too low to sustain them. Such "premature welfare states" then unravel, sending political, social and geopolitical tremors.

D. Gvindadze, *The Transformation of Georgia from 2004 to 2012*, https://doi.org/10.1007/978-3-031-18264-8_10

Political consolidation may reduce horse-trading and broaden margins of maneuver for state builders. Prime minister and ministers of finance do not face pressures from multiple interest groups. This assumes that a ruling political class supports the concept of an efficient government. If not, then weak checks and balances due to the over-consolidation of power may result in bad decisions.

Political consolidation in Georgia in 2004–2012 allowed to structure public spending in line with Georgia's stage of development, avoid social over-promise and earmark maximum resources to infrastructure. Georgia's capital spending (infrastructure spending from budget which fosters long-term growth) as a percentage of total general government expenditure increased from 18.5% in 2004 to more than 20% in all subsequent years. Average annual capital spending in 2004–2012 stood at 22.4% of total general government expenditure. This compares to 9% in Ukraine, 15.2% in Moldova and 19.5% in Armenia.[1] As percent of GDP,

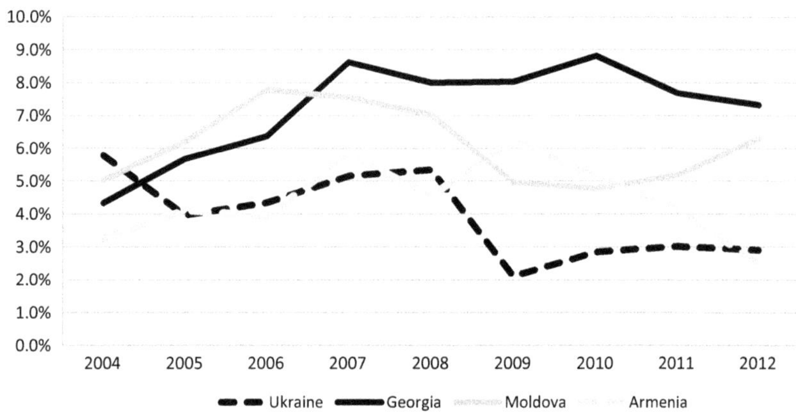

Fig. 10.1 Capital spending in percent of GDP (general government operations, 2004–2012) (*Source* International Monetary Fund. Country reports)

[1] IMF staff reports on Armenia provide information on the central government operations. Because total central government expenditure in these staff reports equals total general government expenditure in the IMF's World Economic Outlook database, I use central government capital expenditure / acquisition of non-financial assets reported in these staff reports to calculate ratios in Figs. 10.1 and 10.2.

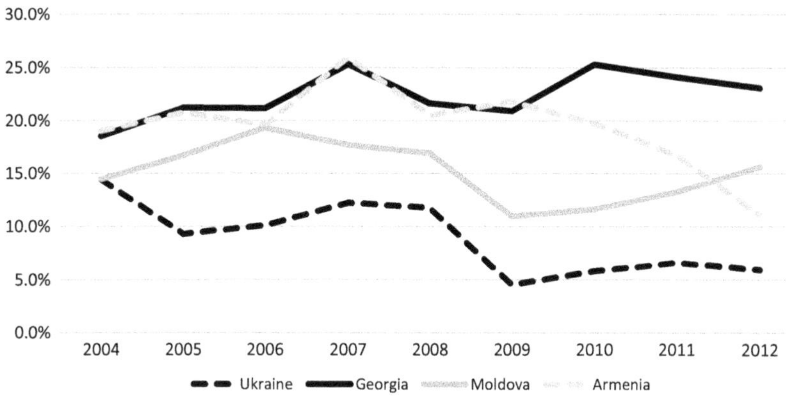

Fig. 10.2 Capital spending in percent of total government expenditure (general government operations, 2004–2012) (*Source* International Monetary Fund. Country reports)

Georgia's capital spending increased from 4.3% in 2004 to approximately 8% in 2007–2012. In 2004–2012, Georgia's average annual capital spending was 7.2% of GDP. This compares to 3.9% in Ukraine, 4.4% in Armenia and 6.1% in Moldova (Figs. 10.1 and 10.2).

This emphasis on infrastructure and control of the recurrent spending in 2004–2012 allowed Georgia to maintain positive government *operating balance* (except in 2009 due to a fiscal response to mitigate the impact of the war with Russia and of the global economic crisis). Post-crisis, Georgia reduced its overall budget deficit faster than planned, from 9.2% of GDP in 2009 to 2.9% of GDP in 2012, committing to its further reduction in 2013. The fiscal consolidation was helped by a fast rebound in confidence: Georgia's real GDP grew by 6.2% in 2010, 7.2% in 2011, and 6.4% in 2012. The fiscal stimulus of 2009–2012 was helped by a fast implementation of infrastructural projects (Box 10.1 and Fig. 10.3).

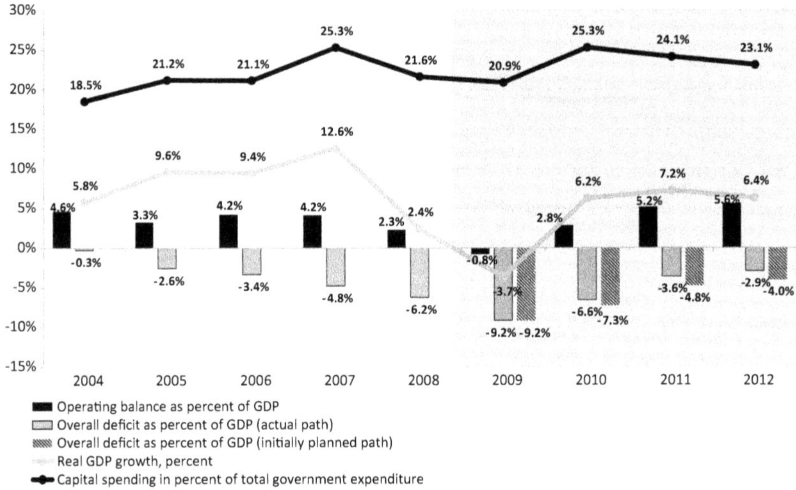

Fig. 10.3 Georgia in 2004–2012: high capital spending and positive operating balances (*Source* Ministry of Finance of Georgia [general government operations GFS 1986])

Box 10.1: Government operating balance in a developing country targeting fast growth

Government operating balance is the difference between a government's recurrent revenues (taxes, other non-tax revenues, grants) and current expenditures (compensation of employees, use of goods and services, subsidies and grants, mandatory social, health and other recurrent expenses, including interest to residents and non-residents). It thus measures the ability to keep in check the current expenditure, including the general government consumption.

A positive operating balance means that a government's recurrent revenues are sufficient to cover its current expenditure, including mandatory spending whose course cannot be changed fast. A strong positive operating balance in a country which runs an insignificant overall budget deficit means that a government is conservative in respect of its current expenditure and that a budget deficit is due to a capital spending (public infrastructure projects). These infrastructure projects are thus funded through a residual generated by subtracting the current expenditure from the recurrent government revenues and through domestic and external public borrowing. If managed cautiously with respect to the public debt dynamics, this is a sound course of action for developing economies. Governments must have solid systems of control to avert cost acceleration, punish embezzlement and prevent "white elephant" projects.

Countries with strong positive operating balances can undertake fiscal consolidation from a position of strength. To reduce budget deficit, they do not need to cut deep into mandatory spending—the exercise which affects livelihoods. They can achieve their goal partly by scaling and sequencing of the capital spending. In times of crises, such countries are rewarded for decoupling their fiscal planning from politics. In contrast, when operating balances are weak or negative, a fiscal consolidation can set a government on a collision course where an abrupt cut of a current spending must happen without jeopardizing political stability while implementing structural reforms to adjust to a new normal.

Georgia's high capital spending was helped by the fast growth and the exchange rate stability, which broadened the sovereign borrowing headroom. Growth enabled infrastructure spending which unlocked new growth opportunities. Public infrastructure projects crowded in private investment and multiplied the impact of the budget spending:

- Enhancement of Georgia's cross-border power transmission network increased investors' interest to construction of hydropower plants in Georgia. Reforms in the energy sector from 2004, an upgrade of a distribution and generation infrastructure allowed to shift from regular blackouts to becoming a net electricity exporter from 2007 (in the context of a strong domestic electricity consumption growth).
- International highways enhanced Georgia's regional logistical and trade function. Local and secondary roads fostered domestic interconnectivity, value added chains and tourism.

- Vertically-integrated comprehensive urban regeneration schemes (where the government identified towns with historic and tourism potential and reengineered their municipal and road infrastructure, beautified facades, revived traditional architecture, developed public spaces and recreation areas) were implemented to help businessmen and local communities to re-discover and invest into economic opportunities of the regenerated sites. This multiplied the impact of the public action. Flagship public projects in Old Tbilisi, Batumi, Sighnaghi, Kutaisi, Telavi, etc., fostered the hospitality industry and created jobs. Georgia has many urban and rural pearls—brand names known throughout former Communist countries and beyond. The task from 2004 was to unearth, regenerate, popularize and multiply them.[2]
- In some cases (new coastal city and deep-sea port in Anaklia, high-altitude ski resorts in Upper Svaneti and Goderdzi, etc.), the government worked to create new growth pockets where entrepreneurs were likelier to follow than to lead. These projects were significant by the Georgian standards and were part of the ambitious spatial planning vision.[3]
- The government worked with internationally acclaimed architects. Positive economics of such projects stretches beyond their immediate costs.

[2] The vertically integrated urban regeneration schemes in Georgia were first pioneered in cooperation with the World Bank. The World Bank's work on territorial development received boost from its 2009 World Development Report "Reshaping Economic Geography" (more on this report and on spatial planning in chapter 17 of this book). By 2009, Georgia had progressed in implementing—with own funds and with support of international development partners—many "horizontal" infrastructure improvement measures: secondary and local roads, highways, water and solid waste management projects. This improved conditions for the mentioned "vertical" approach to urban regeneration. The first World Bank regional development project targeted Kakheti region in Georgia's East and it featured the innovative "vertical" concept which had never been implemented by any international financial institution in Eastern Europe. According to the World Bank (project reports, Regional Development Project, Georgia), this Kakheti project was the first to operationalise the vision put forth by the mentioned 2009 World Development Report. Georgia was invited to the World Bank Headquarters to present its pioneering experience.

[3] For details, see Chapter 17 "Territorial Development and Urbanisation.".

These are what I call *non-contractual* public–private partnerships (somewhat different from *contractual* PPPs explained in Box 10.2). They positioned the government as the catalyst of private investment. Unlike the *contractual* PPPs, they required no formal risk-sharing between the government and private investors and created no hidden budget liabilities.

Box 10.2: Public–Private Partnerships (PPPs) in developing countries and beyond

Contractual PPPs entail *formal* risk-sharing between a project sponsor and a government. For example, in telecom, a government regulates, while telecom companies can be privately owned. In energy, a utility-scale solar power plant developed by a private investor is a transaction with a passthrough from cost of funds to tariff because the investor expects a rate of return. A government may mitigate regulatory and political risks through a government support agreement which creates a contingent fiscal liability but supports an important project promoting green economy transition.

In some cases, risks and benefits of PPPs are less straightforward. Think of an internal rate of return (IRR) on a new international highway project. This IRR cannot be calculated through extrapolation of past traffic volumes. It depends on assumptions on long-term demographic trends, transit flows and regional integration. Many highways are public good projects whose externalities cannot be easily captured in financial models. Unlike the mentioned PPPs in the telecom and energy sectors where governments regulate more than micromanage, in case of highways governments negotiate complex long-term contracts for private sector provision.

PPPs entail creation of project entities which raise project equity and debt. In developing countries, borrowing cost of such project entities is higher than in case of a sovereign borrowing (sovereign lending terms of multilateral development banks are usually uniform across countries of operation, irrespective of such countries' sovereign credit ratings; governments can blend sovereign loans with donor grants to increase concessionality). Higher project cost means higher cost to end-users (car owners) and/or a higher contingent liability for a government.

Complex PPPs require strong public institutions to oversee them. Ministries of finance are the best choice; decentralized management of PPP portfolios amplifies risks. In-house expertise on PPP structuring is lacking in most developing countries' governments, hence need for an expensive external advice. Complex PPPs require "project lifecycle management" techniques, which stretches risk management and administrative capacities.

Fiscal transparency is another consideration. Budget-funded infrastructure projects are reflected upfront in budget deficit and—if funds are borrowed—in public debt. In PPPs, an upfront cost might be incurred by a private sponsor seeking to recover it through user fees or from budget. Fiscal liabilities thus shift into the future. Comparison of the present value of such future liabilities with an upfront cost in case of a budget financing is difficult. An off-budget nature of long-term fiscal liabilities complicates an oversight by parliaments. Infrastructure projects have long repayment periods; hence, initial assumptions might not hold, creating contract renegotiation risks or forcing governments into costly buyouts of project assets.

Bottom line: PPPs play out differently in different sectors, harness PPP opportunities but treat them with caution.

Can a country grow without budget deficits? Singapore's experience in 1990–2018 provides an interesting perspective.[4] Singapore's economy grew from US$ 12,763 in 1990 to US$ 64,579 in 2018, a CAGR of 6%. All along, general government revenues mostly exceeded expenditures (Fig. 10.4).

In public budgeting, countries may shift from libertarianism to socialism. But once socialist (low retirement age, inflated entitlements in civil service, oversized unemployment and medical benefits, etc.) they cannot return back without political tremors. Think of disposable zip tie handcuffs which can be tightened around hands but must be cut to release hands.

[4] IMF estimates of general government revenues and total expenditure start from 1990, hence the look at the period 1990–2018. IMF World Economic Outlook (October 2019).

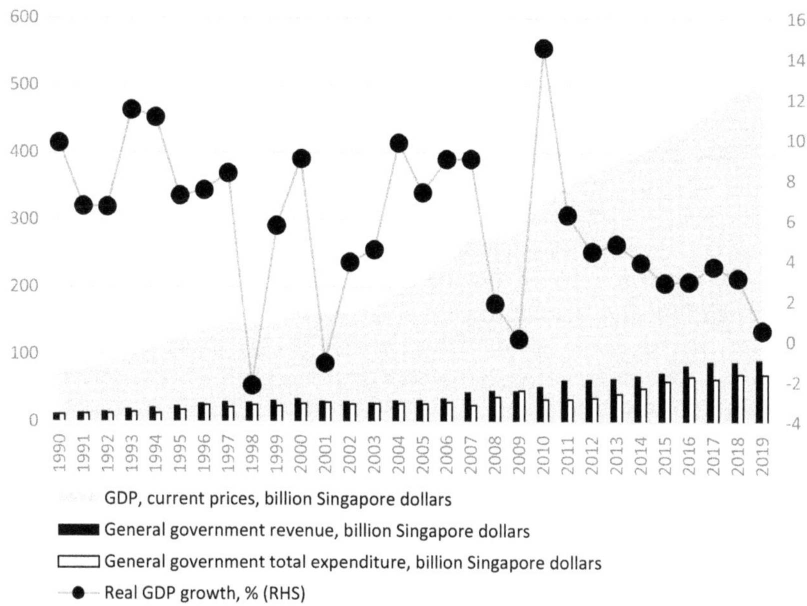

Fig. 10.4 Economic growth and fiscal balance in Singapore in 1990–2018 (*Source* International Monetary Fund. World Economic Outlook [October 2019])

Key to Georgia's focus on infrastructure in 2004–2012 was alignment of public entitlements with fiscal capabilities. Georgia had no automatic indexation of wages, pensions and other benefits. Government consumption was kept under control. As a result of a privatization from 2004, the number of state-owned enterprises (SOEs) was reduced. A handful of remaining SOEs were corporatized and became net contributors to the budget. This removed budget risks associated with opaque SOE sectors. Cost recovery was phased in for municipal services (electricity, gas, water, solid waste). Banks were private and required no budget support. Budget subsidies were low. Budget discipline was generally not disrupted by elections. Pork barrel spending was immaterial. Questions during budget discussions were: to what extend is progress in a given sector dependent on the budget allocation? How much can be outsourced to the private sector? Decision-makers adhered to the principle of not creating public entities—irrespective of how well they fit with a political set-up and how much of an immediate value they add—if there was a risk that in the long run such entities would generate unreasonable quasi-fiscal risks and liabilities, creating a backdoor for mismanagement when political tides change.

In 2004–2012, budget funding played a stronger role in some sectors than in others. The additionality principle whereby public spending *supports* rather than *replaces* private investment was mainly observed. Chapter 11 explains agriculture and healthcare, where a market-based approach entailed reliance on the private sector. Chapter 12 explains public pensions and salaries, where budget funding was key. This approach (do not over-spend in sectors where a real change depends on market forces; earmark budget in sectors where only a government can do a heavy lifting) can foster fiscal optimization and promote a surplus budgeting.

CHAPTER 11

Market-Based Approach in Agriculture and Healthcare

Abstract This chapter explores market-based solutions in agriculture and healthcare. It explains how to modernize and increase productivity in agriculture by harnessing market forces. It explains Georgia's market-based approach to healthcare provision which attracted private investment in hospitals and insurance sector, improved efficiency, sustainability and service quality. It explains the role of growth and wealth accumulation in improving healthcare affordability.

Keywords Agriculture · Employment · Farmers · Healthcare · Hospitals · Insurance

Agriculture

From 2004 to 2005, productivity in Georgia's services and industry sectors increased fast, although in 2012 almost half of the workforce was still locked in agriculture with stagnant productivity, producing approximately one-tenth of the GDP in 2012 (Figs. 11.1 and 11.2).

How to enhance value added per worker in agriculture *and* create productive jobs in industry and services—the two sectors which in advanced economies represent a larger share of employment than in Georgia? How dependent is agricultural productivity on budget spending?

D. Gvindadze, *The Transformation of Georgia from 2004 to 2012*,
https://doi.org/10.1007/978-3-031-18264-8_11

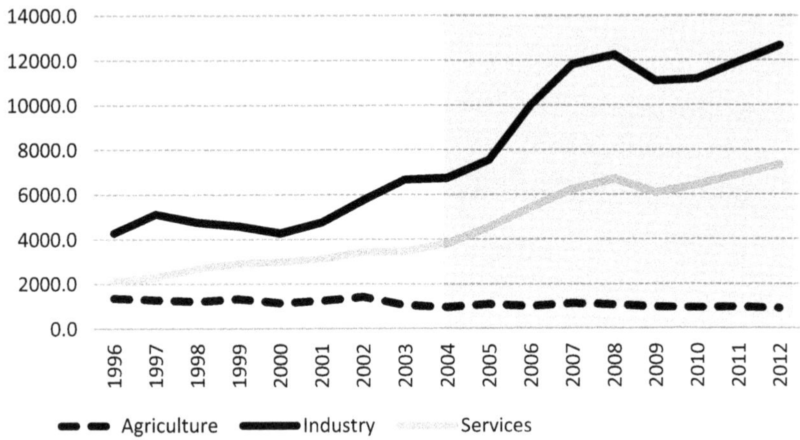

Fig. 11.1 Georgia—labor productivity at constant 1996 prices, GEL (*Source* Geostat)

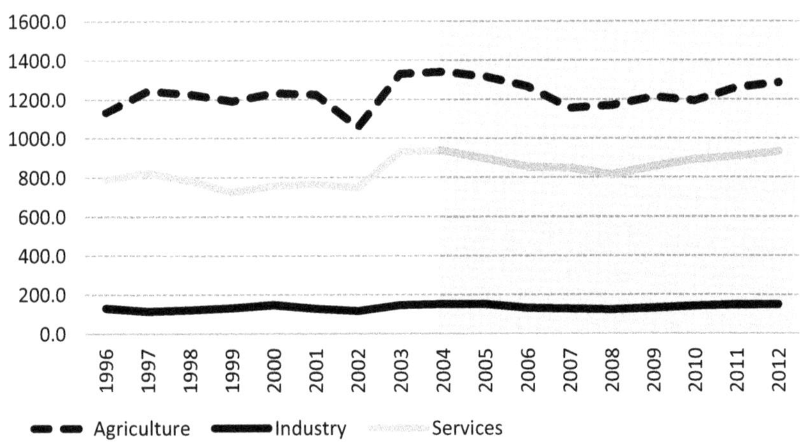

Fig. 11.2 Georgia—employment, in thousand persons (*Source* Geostat)

How big is the role of markets? Can agriculture be discussed in the narrow context of agricultural development, ignoring the state building and modernization?

Below are two thought frameworks. An agricultural development strategy might integrate—for political, social and economic inclusion reasons—elements from the thought framework one. But the problem of low agricultural productivity can be best resolved in a broader context of the thought framework two. Anything short of that might not trigger a structural transformation which Georgia and many developing countries need.

Thought framework one prioritizes budget spending and subsidization. Machinery and irrigation are outdated and in short supply, know-how is missing, arable land is fragmented, farm size is sub-optimal, and elections need to be won. So the government helps, year after year, to seed, plow, cultivate and harvest around one-third of Georgia's land area which is the agricultural land. Welcome as it might be in the short run by subsistence farmers, this thought framework—if not part of the thought framework two—may be rudderless. Can addiction to a heavy agricultural subsidization perpetuate a status quo, reducing, rather than enhancing, the total factor productivity of an economy?

Thought framework two harnesses parallel and consecutive circumstances and events: (1) sound public finances, good business climate and modern banks foster investment, tourism and growth. (2) Growth enhances wealth. (3) Modern food retail and hospitality industries develop. (4) This multiplies vertical retailer- and hospitality business-driven agricultural value added chains. Retailers, restaurants and hotels establish own food processing, canning and farming businesses. This simplifies their supply chain management and allows them to source more products from local farms that they own or back through contract farming arrangements. (5) Local commercial and subsistence farmers enjoy more predictable offtakes. (6) People increasingly treat agriculture as a business. They invest in agriculture to meet a growing domestic demand, harnessing import substitution and export opportunities. (7) Simultaneously, urbanization moves people to cities, a global phenomenon. (8) Proper management of cities and growth improve living conditions and learning opportunities. (9) The ensuing increase in intra-household remittances from urban to rural areas benefits the village. (10) Middle class grows, and so does a demand for local organic products. (11) Commercial and subsistence farmers enjoy increasingly reliable offtakes and higher prices. As their cash flow gets stronger and more predictable, they expand beyond primary agriculture. (12) Lower rural concentration fosters a market-driven agglomeration of small plots into larger commercial farms.[1] A land plot consolidation and commercialization foster private investment in mechanization, irrigation, storage, distribution and export market access infrastructure—something which is too hard in case of a sub-scale production. The causal chain (1)-(12) takes time to materialize, but it is often the most viable causal chain in existence.

In the context of the thought framework two, agriculture is best helped by growth, investment and dynamic cities which provide learning opportunities, attract additional labor force and foster an increase of Georgia's urban population as a percentage of total population.

A similar thinking applies in many other sectors. Big budget spending does not automatically translate into a sustained development and competitiveness. Outcomes often depend on market forces and on multiple other factors.

Healthcare

Ideologically, politically, financially and administratively, healthcare is among the most intricate areas of the public finance. How to transition from the Soviet-era centralized state-run system to a market-based healthcare? How to think of this transition from a public finance perspective? Can it succeed in a vacuum?

At the end of the Soviet Union, a centralized healthcare budget allocation bred corruption and micromanagement across healthcare providers and programs. Hospitals were not businesses, which entailed inefficient operational and capital expenditure planning. The absence of competition among healthcare providers weakened performance incentives and interfered with allocation, training and remuneration of medical, administrative and support staff. Healthcare was formally free, but informal payments were ubiquitous. For complex treatment, families traveled from Georgia to Moscow, with cash and gifts. Renown doctors derived most of revenues from an informal private practice in own apartments. The Communist nomenklatura had access to the best hospitals and sanatoriums.

Georgia's healthcare deteriorated sharply in the 1990s. Budget was under-executed, with in-year budget sequesters. Public health spending

[1] For insights on density of population, urbanization and growth see analytics by the World Bank and McKinsey & Company.

decreased from 4% of GDP in 1991 to 0.59% in 1999. Informal and out-of-pocket payments entailed high costs for households. Nascent insurance industry could not manage healthcare risks and to work with transparent healthcare providers. Low healthcare affordability and Georgia's changed demographic density made many Soviet-era health facilities idle. The number of hospital beds became excessive. Domestic private investment in hospitals was low. Foreign investment was almost zero due to plummeting incomes, bad regulation and corruption. Market-based solutions were mainly failing despite a marginally higher plurality of healthcare provider types and of funding mechanisms.[2]

Discussion on the market-based healthcare gained momentum from 2004. It was helped by Georgia's fast growth, good budget performance, modernizing financial sector, high investment, better regulations and shrinking corruption. The priority was to modernize and optimize the healthcare provision without straining public finances.

In 2007, the government decided to privatize 100 hospitals. It set a total hospital sector capacity and defined locations to ensure a countrywide hospital network accessibility. It introduced new treatment protocols and healthcare provider licensing procedures. The government did not seek big privatization revenues. Private investors were invited to modernize existing facilities in line with pre-set criteria on the understanding that they would replace the state as owners of the facilities and use remaining infrastructure for other commercial aims. In parallel, Georgia introduced healthcare vouchers. Insurance companies (all private) and healthcare providers were to compete to serve state healthcare voucher holders on a lowest cost basis, reflecting in their bids their infrastructure modernization costs. People were free to choose where to redeem their vouchers.

The war with Russia and the global financial crisis from 2008 delayed the process, although the development of a market-based healthcare regained momentum from 2010.

Except the capital Tbilisi which represents almost a half of Georgia's urban population and of GDP, Georgia was divided into healthcare districts. The division was to be temporary—eventually the districts were

[2] Bendukidze et al. (2014).

to lead to a competitive countrywide healthcare marketplace.[3] Insurance companies which by 2007–2010 became better established were invited to compete for serving (as sole healthcare providers) beneficiaries of state-funded health insurance in their chosen healthcare districts *and* to undertake—within two years—to develop, staff and equip new and modernize old hospitals in those districts.

In Tbilisi, many old healthcare facilities were in prime locations. Infrastructurally, they were archaic. The authorities transferred ownership of such facilities to domestic and foreign investors on the condition that they would develop modern hospitals in pre-agreed areas of Tbilisi and in Georgia's regions. This helped to regenerate land plots and buildings where old facilities were located and to develop modern medical clusters in and beyond Tbilisi. Tbilisi's economic and demographic dominance allowed a broader set of hospital privatization schemes than in regions where insurers developed infrastructure assuming temporary geographic monopolies.

Most of the public healthcare spending was channeled through insurance companies which provided healthcare packages to people below poverty line, to teachers, internally displaced persons in their areas of resettlement and to communities close to the occupied territories. Focus on the means testing diversified the insured population. These were old and weak for whom vouchers would be expensive due to high health risks and young and poor whose lower health risks allowed to reduce per-voucher price paid by the government to insurance companies. Insurance companies, of which some were integrated into financial holdings, were privately owned. This reduced the government ownership of healthcare facilities, except for less commercially attractive disease control and prevention hospitals.

Insurance companies' move into the healthcare provision led to their vertical integration with healthcare service providers. Interactions between rapidly expanding pharmaceutical chains, private insurance companies, private hospitals and beneficiaries of the state healthcare insurance (who co-participate in healthcare costs to avert over-spending) introduced checks and balances, with the parties watching after each other to avoid being ripped off. It also created collusion risks (e.g., when an insurance company builds a regional hospital serving its policyholders)

[3] N. Gilauri (2017).

to mitigate which the authorities applied moral suasion, protocols and inspections.

By 2013, private investors built up to 150 modern hospitals and clinics in Georgia. Almost all hospitals were transferred into private ownership, with 40% of hospitals owned by insurance companies, 30% by individuals and 20% by other types of enterprises.[4] Anchor hospitals providing multiple services were linked to healthcare providers with a narrower range of services. Commercial viability of the healthcare improved. Consolidation ensued and foreign investment increased. Corruption and informal payments decreased. Healthcare providers started competing on quality of infrastructure, staff, patient management and equipment. Some started positioning themselves as medical tourism destinations. The healthcare sector started paying taxes. The state healthcare insurance expanded from 196,000 beneficiaries in September 2006 to 740,000 in April 2008 and to 2.1 million from September 2012. In 2012, almost half of Georgia's population thus received state-funded health insurance vouchers. Such insurance market increase was notable, bearing in mind that in 2006 health insurance beneficiaries' cohort was limited to around 100,000 Tbilisi residents.[5] Enrollment in private health insurance increased from 40,000 persons in 2009 to 450,000 persons in 2012.[6] Fast forward into 2015 and Georgia Healthcare Group (GHG)—Georgia's largest vertically integrated healthcare services and medical insurance provider—announced admission of its entire ordinary share capital to the premium listing at the London Stock Exchange (LSE). GHG remains the only LSE-listed healthcare group in the region.

Challenges remained: out-of-pocket healthcare expenditure was a risk to households across income levels; profitability of certain hospitals was weak and depended on the regional service provision monopolies.

Economic growth enhances healthcare affordability and improves healthcare outcomes. Fast wealth accumulation is key to improved lives and livelihoods. A competitive medical tourism industry can cross-subsidize health access for Georgia's citizens.

[4] The Georgian Hospital Sector, Transparency International Georgia (2012) https://www.transparency.ge/sites/default/files/post_attachments/TIG%20Hospital%20report%20_5%20Jul_%20final.pdf (retrieved in June 2020).

[5] Ibid.

[6] Bendukidze et al. (2014).

CHAPTER 12

Pensions and Public Sector Salaries

Abstract This chapter takes a cross-country look at public and private pensions. It explains pension system in Georgia in 2004–2012 and discusses applicability of a pension system's five pillars. It explains public employees' compensation and the role of salaries, agile reward mechanisms and other factors in motivating civil servants.

Keywords Pension · Saving · Subsistence minimum · Salary

Pensions

Pension systems are influenced by electoral cycles, social contracts, economic constraints and goals. Fiscal footprint, composition and complexity of pension systems vary. Figure 12.1 shows *public* pension spending as percent of GDP for countries at different levels of GDP per capita in 2012. We see (1) a significant divergence in magnitudes of the public pension spending as share of GDP and (2) no strong correlation between GDPs per capita and ratio of the public pension spending to GDP. In 2012, *private* pension spending (consists of payments made to private pension plan members, or dependents after retirement and covers persons working in both public and private sectors) varied, for example,

D. Gvindadze, *The Transformation of Georgia from 2004 to 2012*,
https://doi.org/10.1007/978-3-031-18264-8_12

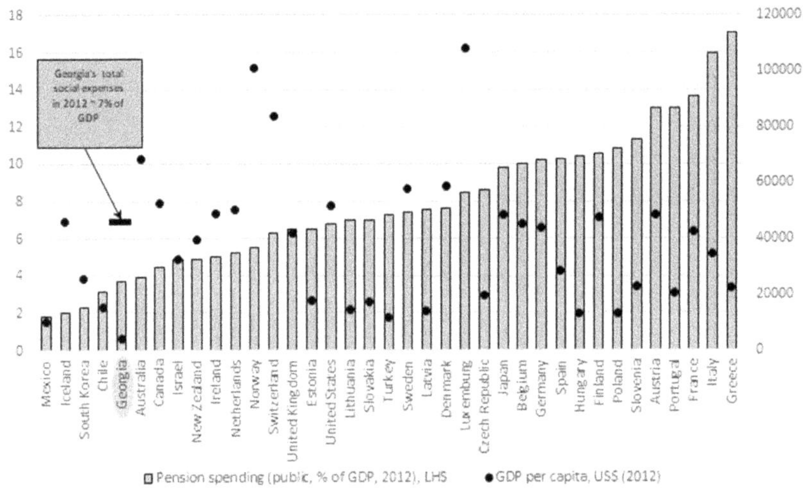

Fig. 12.1 GDP per capita and public pension spending as percent of GDP in 2012 (*Source* OECD (2022), Pension spending (indicator). https://doi.org/10.1787/a041f4ef-en (Accessed on 12 August). International Monetary Fund. World Economic Outlook Database (October 2019). International Monetary Fund Country Report No. 12/98 (Georgia), April 2012)

from almost 5% in Iceland and Denmark to almost zero in Albania and Romania.[1]

The World Bank's conceptual framework for pension reform includes 5 pillars[2]:

1. A non-contributory zero pillar (a social pension paid from budget to ensure minimum social protection for the elderly).
2. A mandatory first pillar (pension contributions related to earnings, usually funded on a pay-as-you-go basis which subjects the pillar to political and demographic risks).

[1] OECD Social Expenditure: Aggregated Data, Pension Spending, Private. The database defines pension spending as all cash expenditures on old-age and survivor's pensions.

[2] World Bank Pension Reform Primer 45728, "The World Bank Pension Conceptual Framework" http://documents.worldbank.org/curated/en/389011468314712045/pdf/457280BRI0Box31Concept1Sept20081pdf.pdf (retrieved in January 2019).

3. A mandatory second pillar (typically a defined contribution personal saving account managed by a fund manager, where such individual contribution by employees can be matched with contributions from an employer and from a budget).
4. A voluntary third pillar (discretionary, depends on an individual's ability to save).
5. A non-financial fourth pillar (includes family, health and housing support).

In 2004–2012, Georgia had a non-contributory zero pillar (pensions paid from a general budget revenue pool—the de facto old-age safety net), a voluntary third pillar (voluntary savings, mainly in banks) and a non-financial fourth pillar (family support, certain government healthcare benefits and insurance). Georgia had no state pension funds. Social benefits and pensions were paid from a general budget (social tax was abolished from 2008, as explained in Chapter 14). This allowed to avoid costs of administration of such pension funds and to explicitly reflect pension liabilities in the budget. Complex pension funds in developing countries at times run annual deficits; governments are forced to come to their rescue.

In 2004, monthly old-age pensions in Georgia (zero-pillar old-age safety net) stood at GEL 14 (US$ 7.32 at current exchange rate), well below the subsistence minimum (Fig. 12.2). Ten pension increases occurred in 2004–2013. Old-age pensions exceeded the subsistence minimum for the first time in 2013 when—based on the 2013 budget prepared in 2012—pensions increased to GEL 150 (US$ 90.36 at current exchange rate). In real (average consumer price inflation-adjusted) terms, pensions in 2004–2012 increased 6.5 times.

Special pensions and early retirement schemes in 2004–2012 were fiscally immaterial and applied to a limited number of beneficiaries. Pensions were not indexed to inflation. Pension increases were driven by Georgia's economic fundamentals. Regular retirement age was 65 years for men and 60 years for women (Georgia's life expectancy at birth is 67.5 years for men and 75.4 years for women).[3] Equalization of the retirement ages did not happen as this would hit people with no formal employment for whom old-age pensions were the main revenue.

[3] Geostat (life expectancy at birth, 2021).

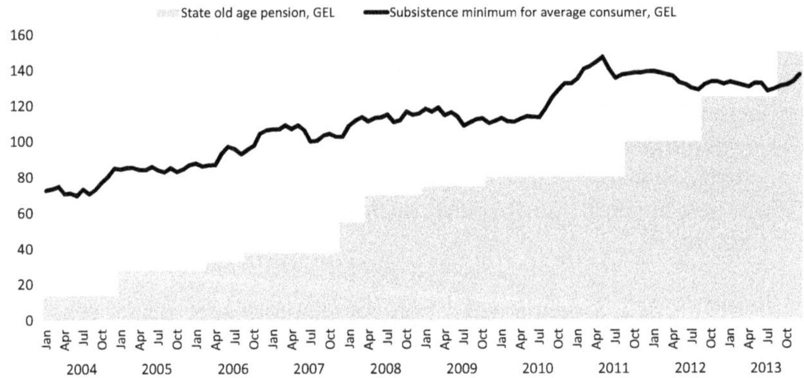

Fig. 12.2 State old-age pensions and subsistence minimum in Georgia, 2004–2013 (*Source* Geostat)

In 2012, the government discussed—but did not enact—the mandatory second pillar. It was deemed premature. Note that according to the World Bank "Some of the ... societies may find that mandated first and second pillar schemes present obstacles to increased formalization of the labor force and achieve better outcomes with a combination of a social pension and a more extensive voluntary system."[4]

The mandatory second pillar may help to (1) improve a post-retirement quality of life, (2) increase domestic savings, which is important given Georgia's dependence on foreign capital, a negative current account (current account deficit is difference between saving and investment) and a negative net international investment position (difference between international assets and liabilities of a country), (3) replace part of consumption with investment, (4) create GEL-denominated liquidity for local commercial banks and for the government borrowing and support de-dollarization and (5) foster domestic capital market development, with pension fund manager(s) as institutional investor(s) with long-term investment horizon.

[4] World Bank Pension Reform Primer 45728, "The World Bank Pension Conceptual Framework".

In practice, an introduction of the mandatory second pillar in a small open low- to middle-income developing economy must be preceded by a discussion of the following:

- Is an introducing government (or a government-hired pension fund) a better investor than private citizens mandated to contribute to the second pillar from their earnings?
- What are long-term investment opportunities and instruments in an introducing country and do they allow to absorb an increasing cumulative pool of the mandatory pension savings? Can local firms issue adequately rated corporate bonds? Can local banks absorb more local currency deposits without incurring costs of carry when demand for credit is low? If not, what are pros and cons of investing in government securities? If the latter happens, is a government a more efficient spender than individuals? What is the prospect of supply of such government securities? Can the urge to park an increasing pool of pension savings into government securities conflict with fiscal consolidation which entails a reduced borrowing and thus a reduced supply of such government securities?
- Assuming that an introducing country's sovereign credit rating is in a sub-investment category, this establishes a sub-investment "sovereign ceiling" for its banks and corporates. Is it appropriate to "expose" mandatory contributors by investing their retirement savings long-term into high-risk assets?
- Developing country politics is often unpredictable. Not much is sacrosanct in the long run. Responsible governments may be replaced by populists. How ironclad are legal, political and institutional safeguards which prevent future governments from using the mandatory savings for their own political needs?
- If invested domestically, how protected is the real value of the mandatory savings in a small open economy where inflation is influenced by external factors and the exchange rate stability depends on inbound foreign investment, lending and remittances?
- To what extent can state pension funds' investments outside an introducing country pressure its exchange rate? Do investments into foreign investment-grade securities have adequate yields?

- How does a pension reform fit into domestic capital market development? Which are small developing country examples of a positive time-tested correlation between the mandatory second pillar, de-dollarization and local capital markets development?
- Are employers contributing to the mandatory second pillar together with beneficiaries and the state ready for it administratively, legally and financially? Can additional bureaucracy deter employment and foster informality?
- Current account balance is the difference between savings and investment (if a country invests more than it saves, it runs a current account deficit). Can a mandatory increase in savings help with external rebalancing of an economy? Or, does external rebalancing materialize through high investment changing structure of an economy and lifting it to a higher equilibrium (in contrast to a lower equilibrium in case of an import compression through forced savings)?
- Are poor individuals spending on basic necessities ready to forego current consumption in exchange for a promise of an enhanced future social safety?
- In contrast to a defined benefit scheme, defined contribution scheme means that a government—or a government-hired fund manager—is not liable for losses in real value of savings. In practice, because the mandatory pillar is introduced by a government, a government bears an ultimate political responsibility for maintenance and enhancement of the real value of savings. This might lead to government-led bailouts, quasi-fiscal outlays and losses.
- Is the mandatory pillar contribution a new implicit tax? As explained in Chapter 14 (tax reform section), Georgia's Liberty Act of 2011 obliged the government to submit to a referendum an introduction of new national taxes (except excise) or an increase of existing tax rates. Even if an employee's contribution is not a tax (because it increases threefold due to a matching from an employer and a government and an employee recovers funds upon retirement), can an employer's and a government's contributions be interpreted as a new tax?
- How can individuals withdraw their pension savings, accrued capital gains and interest before a retirement age?

- Can private savings be increased voluntarily via commercial banks, through tailor-made products and awareness raising campaigns (i.e., a voluntary third pillar)?
- The mandatory second pillar entails a new state agency and a new fund manager(s) executing an investment policy. How much do these entities cost and how would this affect an effective rate of return on investments? How to ring-fence these entities from manipulation? How will fund managers incentivize long-term returns?
- If participation in the mandatory second pillar applies to individuals below a certain age, can employers' preferences tilt to hiring older people, which would foster youth employment?
- How complex is legal and tax-related guidance to companies and individuals shifting to the mandatory second pillar (think of types of employment contracts, of short-term expert and consultant contracts where arrangements must be easy and fast)?
- Can a higher cost to an employer reduce formal employment and salaries? Can an employer pressure an employee into accepting a lower salary to recover costs? Does a contributing government benefit higher salary earners disproportionately because (1) a government's contribution represents a fixed share of a salary and (2) even if such share reduces with an increase in salary such reductions might lack granularity? Will the thresholds for reduction of a government's contribution be changing with salaries' growth, inflation and exchange rate? Which adjustment mechanisms will apply and how onerous will their complexity be?
- Can it be more efficient for a government of a small developing country to focus mostly on a non-contributory zero pillar where a pension is adjusted to budget constraints and guarantees a subsistence minimum for all?

Developments in Europe in 2014–2016 illustrate complexities of sustaining a long-term real value of savings. Georgian Lari (GEL) depreciated against US$ by 34% in 2014–2016.[5] Reasons behind the

[5] From 2004 till 2012, the period focused on in this book, Georgian Lari (GEL) appreciated against the US$ by close to 20%, from approximately 2.1 GEL per US$ in the beginning of 2004 to approximately 1.66 GEL per US$ at the end of 2012. Within this nine-year period, GEL's appreciation against US$ lasted from 2004 till end

depreciation were internal (polarized politics) and external: (1) Russia's war against Ukraine from 2014; (2) an ensuing 70% depreciation of Ukraine's hryvnia against US$ in 2014–2016 and a deep recession in Ukraine where real GDP contracted by 6.6% in 2014 and 10% in 2015 (Ukraine is Georgia's important trade partner); (3) an economic and geopolitical impact of sanctions and countersanctions between Russia and the West in 2014–2016; (4) a concurrent fall in oil price from more than US$ 100 per barrel in the beginning of 2014 to US$ 30 per barrel in the beginning of 2016 which triggered an almost 50% depreciation of the Russian ruble against US$ in 2014–2016 and forced Russia into recession, with its real GDP contracting by 3.7% in 2015 and 0.76% in 2016; (5) a knock-on impact of the currency depreciation and recession in Russia on Belarus which depends on Russia for trade and subsidies (Belarus ruble depreciated against US$ by 50% in 2014–2016 and Belarus's real GDP contracted for three years in a row in 2015–2017) and on other neighboring countries which maintain with Russia trade, investment and financial ties; (6) pressures created by the low oil prices on Azerbaijan, due to its reliance on export of hydrocarbons (Azerbaijan's economy contracted in 2016 and Azerbaijani manat was step-devalued against US$ by 56% in 2014–2016 to rebalance the economy externally and internally and to restore competitiveness).

This web of interdependencies surrounds Georgia and its trade and investment partners. It is complicated by the volatility of Turkish lira (in 2016, Turkey accounted for 8% of Georgia's exports and 15% of imports). Can a government or a government-hired pension fund preserve and enhance a real value of the mandatory second pillar savings when these are invested long term in a complex political, economic and geopolitical context?

Discussions on pensions in early stage developing countries must integrate several principles: (1) complexity creates millionaires in banks' structured finance units, but in immature public sectors it may trigger risks which officials cannot handle across electoral cycles; hence simplicity is good. (2) Rapid growth and good governance are important. This

of October 2008, at which point GEL depreciated against US$ due to Georgia's war with Russia and the global financial crisis. This depreciation lasted till mid-2010, at which point GEL appreciation re-started.

fosters pension system sustainability by improving health and demographics, enhances formal and informal employment, increases incomes, intra-household and inter-generational support mechanisms, broadens tax base and lengthens planning horizons for individuals and businesses. This strengthens the fourth pillar of the pension system and beefs up the third pillar as, beyond traditional bank deposits, excess cash can be saved through online traders facilitating debt and equity exposures. (3) A zero pillar ensuring a minimum old-age social protection should continue to be funded through general budget. (4) Fiscal prudence is important because once locked in pension entitlements cannot be undone.

Public Sector Salaries

Public employees' attitudes are not shaped by salaries alone. But inadequate salaries dent enthusiasm and contribute to a reform fatigue and to an abuse of public office. Good salaries attract talent but also breed a question: *why is a minister paid better than a pensioner?* Governments answer or dodge this question differently. If a government is successful and instills trust, this question loses some of its armor-piercing abilities.

A sustained increase in salaries can only happen on the back of an increase in tax revenues. Donors can be asked to chip in to kick off reforms, but this support cannot be indefinite. Otherwise, you create a parallel universe of well-paid people rendering technical support to officials who wield real powers. This can add marginal value but will not be a game changer.

Any state building depends on a core team of reformers. Even when fiscal constraints bind, such teams do not cost too much. Imagine a low-income country of 5 million inhabitants at GDP per capita of US$ 2,000, which translates into a GDP of US$10 billion. Assume government size at 30% of GDP, so a public budget of US$ 3 billion. Assume a 500 person-strong core team tasked with spearheading important reforms. Assume further that to monthly base salaries of these individuals we add a US$ 2,000 monthly bonus. This means a total monthly budget outlay of US$ 1 million, or US$ 12 million annually. This is 0.4% of the annual budget. Spending this sum to trigger a breakthrough is fiscally achievable and it is a good idea. Note that the base salaries are approved by cabinets and parliaments as part of laws on civil service and public administration, whereas ministers can pay the bonuses at their discretion within their annual budget ceilings. Bonuses might even exceed base salaries. This set-up rewards performance and precludes irreversible fiscal commitments.

Figure 12.3 shows earnings in Georgia's public administration. Growth and stable exchange rate fostered an increase in nominal and real inflation-adjusted earnings.

Figure 12.4 provides a cross-country comparison of compensation of employees as percent of government expense in 2012. Georgia is in the middle of the distribution. The ratio for Georgia remained almost unchanged in 2004–2012 when growth of salaries followed growth of tax revenues. The share of public sector employment in Georgia's total employment decreased from 20.6% in 2006 to 15.9% in 2012.

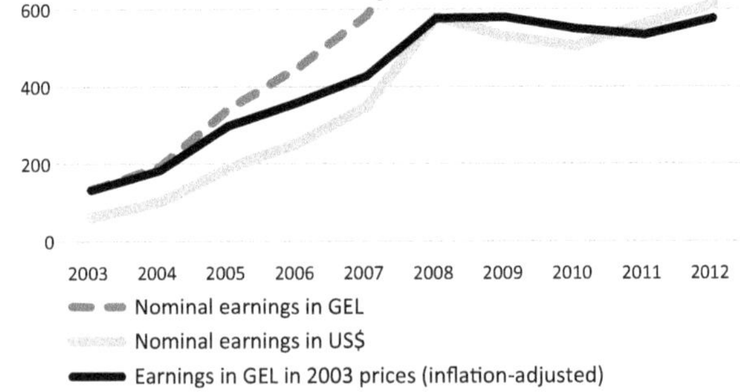

Fig. 12.3 Nominal and real monthly earnings in Georgia's public administration in 2003–2012 (*Source* Geostat, national Bank of Georgia, own calculations)

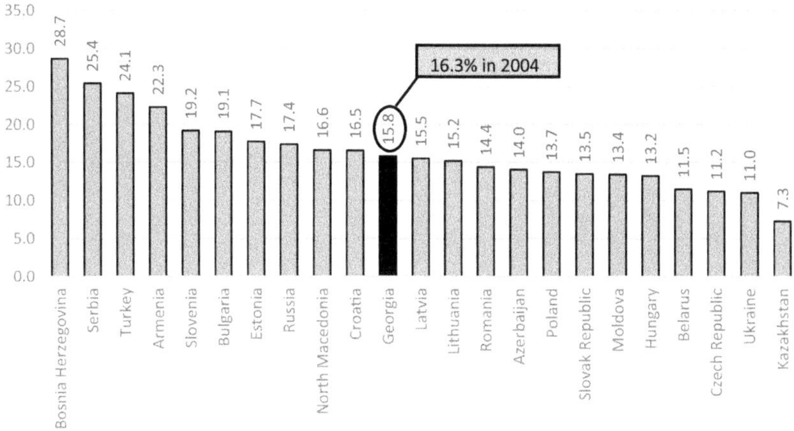

* Compensation of employees consists of all payments in cash, as well as in kind (such as food and housing), to employees in return for services rendered, and government contributions to social insurance schemes such as social security and pensions that provide benefits to employees.

Fig. 12.4 Compensation of employees*, percent of expense in 2012, regional perspective (*Source* International Monetary Fund. Government Finance Statistics Yearbook and data files [May 2020])

CHAPTER 13

Public Debt, Capital Markets and International Assistance

Abstract This chapter discusses Georgia's public debt in 2004–2012 and institutional, procedural and legal factors influencing decisions and outcomes. It explores public debt-related risks and mitigation strategies. It discusses trade-offs between borrowing from international development partners and capital markets. It explores how a sovereign's access to international capital markets can attract private investment and explains work with international development partners.

Keywords Public debt · International assistance · Capital markets · Eurobond

Public Debt Management in Georgia in 2004–2012—Outcomes, Risks and Trade-Offs

Public debt sustainability is important for an uninterrupted economic growth. A public debt reduction is an uphill task. It can be accomplished

D. Gvindadze, *The Transformation of Georgia from 2004 to 2012*,
https://doi.org/10.1007/978-3-031-18264-8_13

through growth, debt restructuring or fiscal adjustment.[1] Challenges abound.

- Growth can reduce debt as a share of GDP and of budget expenditure. This can happen when nominal GDP growth (a product of growth of volume of production and of price inflation) outstrips interest paid on debt. A narrow economic base in developing countries usually entails deeper peak-to-trough contractions. A regular recurrence of crises leaves no time to repair sovereign and corporate balance sheets. For example, over the last quarter century, Georgia was affected by the Russian financial crisis in 1998, Turkish economic crisis of 2001, global financial crisis of 2007–2009, Russian invasion into Georgia in 2008, European sovereign debt crisis from 2009, Russian invasion into Ukraine from 2014, Turkish currency crisis in 2019 and the COVID-19 crisis from 2020. Oil price decreases hit oil producers and impact their neighbors through trade, remittances, investment and exchange rate channels.
- Sovereign debt restructuring entails long discussions with official lenders and private investors into sovereign bonds. Transaction costs are significant. Even a reprofiling of public debt (which leaves principal value of debt intact but changes its present value through deferred payments) takes time. International financial institutions usually do not restructure their loans due to their "preferred creditor" status (except in cases of coordinated debt write-offs for poor countries). A reduction of a principal amount of public debt owed to private sector creditors might involve painful trade-offs like GDP-linked warrants related to a debtor's future growth. A restructuring sovereign makes negative headlines and is downgraded by rating agencies to a default category. This scares off investors. Deterioration of a sovereign risk hits domestic firms and banks, multiplying the damage.
- Fiscal adjustments entail a tax increase and/or a decrease of spending. Both are difficult. To boost foreign and domestic investment, many developing countries need low taxes. A spending

[1] The Economist's Briefing "Covid-19 and public finances" (25 April 2020) discusses the public debt implications of the COVID-19 pandemic and the hard choices and trade-offs it forces on the world. The analysis below elaborates on some of the same choices and trade-offs in a developing country context.

decrease disrupts livelihoods and might not help without a private sector-led rebound. Economic crises usually result in more spending to address widened income gaps. The COVID-19 crisis may result in permanently high healthcare costs and structural deficits.

- Developing countries have an "original sin" problem. Much of their external debt is denominated in hard currencies which in crises appreciate against national currencies. A balance of payments deficit and a negative net international investment position (a difference between a country's international assets and liabilities) in a small, open and dollarized developing country enhance its vulnerability to currency devaluations and to adverse balance sheet effects which trigger abrupt increases of debt service costs.
- Even low stock of public debt may disguise risks. Private sector bailouts strain public finances. Public borrowing may spike to close fiscal and external funding gaps. International capital markets may inhibit refinancing of external liabilities. Local capital markets may be too shallow to replace external borrowing and to remain liquid in times of stress. Developing economies have a narrow economic base, so crises cause large swings in output, with spikes in debt to GDP ratios driven by adverse denominator effects.
- Retirement of a hard currency-denominated external public debt by tapping domestic capital market is complex: (1) external debt for infrastructure projects is difficult to retire before maturity due to legal and procurement-related technicalities. (2) Domestic capital markets in developing countries are too shallow to close fiscal and external funding gaps during crises. (3) Securing cheap money in domestic capital markets might require a strong "moral suasion" or a "financial repression" entailing excessive intrusion.
- Developing countries' monetary policies are constrained. For example, a quantitative easing through central bank purchases of treasuries and of corporate debt drove interest rates to zero in advanced economies. But in small developing countries with immature institutions, a quantitative easing can amplify "moral hazard" and increase inflation without clear exit strategies. High inflation in the context of a low productivity dents competitiveness through a real effective exchange rate appreciation. This might lead to a depreciation of a nominal exchange rate which in dollarized developing countries increases a public debt to GDP ratio and a public debt service to budget revenues ratio.

- Interest payment on external debt is sensitive to base rate fluctuations and in case of bonds to rollover terms. Global interest rate benchmarks may go up, increasing debt service costs even if contractual spreads over such benchmarks are fixed. For example, the London Interbank Offered Rate (LIBOR) is a reference rate setting the base price of loan agreements worth trillions of dollars.[2] LIBOR went from close to 7% in mid-2000 to almost 1% in mid-2003 to more than 5% in the fall of 2006 before falling again to less than 1% toward the end of 2009. Interest rates on sovereign, sub-sovereign, quasi-sovereign and private sector loans to developing countries represent a sum of LIBOR and a credit margin. Unless the interest rate is fixed (which entails an additional cost), borrowers are exposed to LIBOR and credit margin fluctuations.

Prime ministers and ministers of finance who limit public borrowing are often (unsung) heroes. Some are good at communicating their constraints internally and to external creditors. Others fail the communication part and end up misunderstood. Failure to engage with external creditors may push such creditors into discussions with more government counterparts, complicating a ministry of finance's task.

No uniform set of debt sustainability metrics can be applied to countries at different stages of development. A 60% public debt to GDP ceiling in the Treaty of Maastricht for countries adopting the Euro is a poor yardstick for small developing countries with lower "debt intolerance thresholds."[3] A target ratio of 25–30% is more reasonable. Imagine a country with a public debt stock of US$ 300 (all denominated in US$, courtesy of the "original sin" problem) and GDP of 2000 local currency units (LCU). If 2 LCUs equal 1 US$, then a "peacetime" pre-crisis public debt to GDP ratio is 30%. Now imagine a crisis situation. Assume that a country needs to borrow US$ 100 for its balance of payment or fiscal needs, which increases the public debt stock to US$ 400. Assume that a real GDP falls by 5%, inflation is 5% and the exchange rate depreciates by one-third so that 1 US$ becomes equal to 3 LCUs. The public debt to

[2] Recent claims of manipulation of the LIBOR setting process has led to investigations and work to replace LIBOR.

[3] In response to the COVID-19 crisis from 2020, the EU suspended its fiscal rules by which countries are expected to reduce their debt to GDP ratios to 60%.

GDP ratio doubles from 30 to 60%, weakening the immunity to future crises.[4]

Public debt sustainability was, therefore, key to Georgia's growth and FDI push strategy in 2004–2012. It materialized through:

- Engagement with multilateral and bilateral development banks which practice transparent untied procurement, support project implementation and assess public debt sustainability implications of their loans.
- Conservative assessment of a risk profile of public debt portfolio and attention to flatness of the debt redemption path to avert refinancing risks.
- Limited exposure to non-concessional public debt and to floating rates; achievement of high concessionality through blending of long-term loans from multilateral and bilateral development banks with grants from the European Union and bilateral donors.
- Almost zero exposure to "tied" loans due to their hidden costs (an effective interest rate of a tied loan can exceed an interest rate in a loan agreement because of a borrower government's limited leverage in price negotiations between a creditor government and a company from the creditor country which is entrusted with delivery of goods and services under the loan agreement).
- The absence of direct or contingent sovereign guarantees (public debt incurred directly by the Ministry of Finance representing Georgia).
- Limited indebtedness of state-owned enterprises, with limited contingent liabilities for the sovereign.
- The absence of state-owned banks and hence of directed or subsidized lending by such banks (which might result in quasi-fiscal liabilities).
- Avoidance of direct borrowing by sub-sovereign entities (public debt incurred by the Ministry of Finance on-lending to sub-sovereign entities at low or zero risk margin or transferring funds without a repayment obligation). Multilateral development banks usually lend to central governments at same low rates irrespective of sovereign

[4] $(300 + 100)/((2000*(1-0.05)*(1 + 0.05))/3) = 0.6 = 60\%$

credit ratings of such governments, whereas lending terms to municipalities are risk-driven and higher. From an integrated public finance perspective, Georgia preferred to borrow on a sovereign basis and then onlend or transfer funds to municipalities.

- Strict ban on monetization of budget deficits by the central bank.
- Public debt management legislation precluding individual discretion and ensuring cross-scrutiny.
- Cautious approach to accessing international debt markets (discussed later in this chapter) (Fig. 13.1).

In 2003–2007, public debt to GDP ratio decreased from 63.2 to 25.5%, helped by economic growth and conservative borrowing. The low public debt to GDP ratio in the first half of 2008 and flat debt redemption path allowed to implement, in 2008–2009, a fiscal stimulus which returned Georgia to growth from 2010. Public debt peaked at 42.4% of GDP in 2010 and decreased to 34.9% by 2012. Simultaneously, external

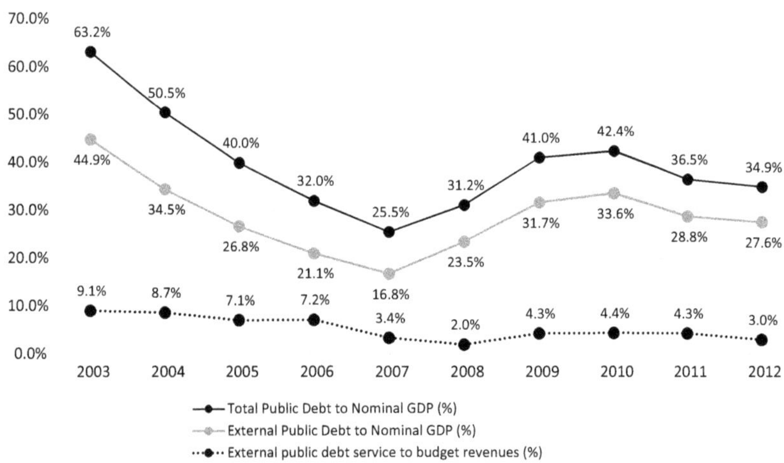

Fig. 13.1 Georgia's public debt stock and flow ratios, 2003–2012 (*Source* Statistical bulletin of the public debt of Georgia N1-December 2013. Ministry of Finance of Georgia, https://mof.ge/images/File/debt-bulletin/Public-Sector-Debt-Statistical-Bulletin-N1_GEO-Final.pdf [retrieved in October 2020])

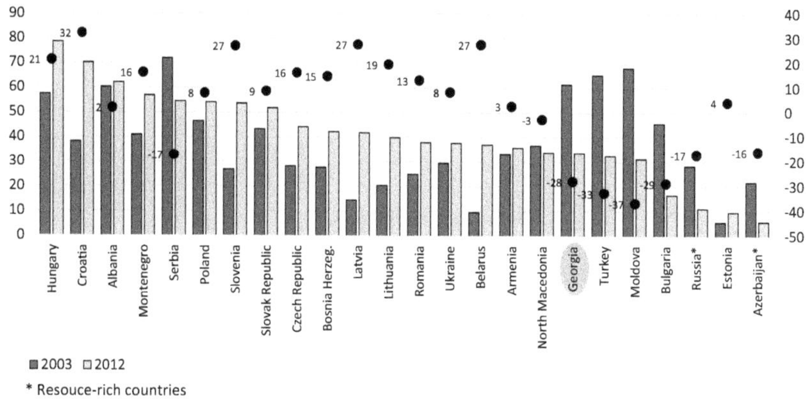

Fig. 13.2 General government gross debt, percent of GDP in 2003 and 2012 (*Source* International Monetary Fund. World Economic Outlook [October 2020])

public debt to GDP ratio decreased to 27.6% in 2012 (Fig. 13.2).[5] At 61% in 2003, Georgia's general government debt to GDP ratio was among the highest in the region whereas at 33% in 2012 it was among the lowest (Fig. 13.3).

Georgia's public debt structure evolved in 2004–2012. Concessional long-term debt to multilateral and bilateral development partners increased while the share of a short-term non-concessional debt (including "historic debt" incurred in the 1990s) decreased (Table 13.1). At the end of 2012, 73% of Georgia's external public debt stock had fixed interest rate and 27% had a variable rate, which limited exposure to base rate fluctuations.[6] "Grant element" (a degree of concessionality of a

[5] In Georgia, the difference between domestic and external public debt is based on the currency of denomination. Domestic public debt is GEL-denominated, owed largely to local residents and governed by the domestic law. External public debt is denominated in foreign currencies, owed to foreign residents and governed by foreign laws. The currency of denomination-based definition thus ensures de facto consistency across all standard economic and legal definitions of difference between domestic and external public debt.

[6] Ministry of Finance of Georgia, Statistical Bulletin of Public Debt of Georgia N1, December 2013. https://mof.ge/images/File/debt-bulletin/Public-Sector-Debt-Statistical-Bulletin-N1_GEO-Final.pdf (retrieved in October 2020).

Table 13.1 Georgia's public debt stock structure, end-2012

	2012 (%)
External public debt (% of total public debt)	**79**
o/w Multilateral	55
Bilateral	13
Eurobond	10
Domestic public debt (% of total public debt)	**21**
o/w "historic" debt	7

Source Ministry of Finance of Georgia, Statistical Bulletin N1 of Public Debt of Georgia (December 2013)

loan) of Georgia's public debt portfolio increased.[7] In 2012, weighted average interest rate on Georgia's public external debt stock was less than 2%. Refinancing and market risks were reduced. In 2004–2012, Georgia was top performer in the Country Policy and Institutional Assessments of the World Bank and the Asian Development Bank. This boosted performance-based eligibility for cheap funding from the International Development Association (part of the World Bank) and from the Asian Development Fund (Asian Development Bank).

As Georgia was developing its domestic public debt market in 2010–2012, macroeconomic discipline helped to reduce yields across all maturities of treasuries and to extend maturity of treasuries from 2 to 10 years. Weighted average maturity of the treasuries' portfolio increased from 0.9 years in 2011 to 2.2 years in 2012. Weighted average interest rate of the treasuries' portfolio decreased from 11.6% in 2011 to 9.1% in 2012.[8] Increase in the stock of treasuries in 2010–2012 happened in small steps. In 2012, it represented 6% of Georgia's public debt stock and 2% of GDP—a low ratio compared to advanced countries which rely more on

[7] The grant element is defined as the difference between a loan's nominal value (face value) and the sum of the discounted future debt-service payments to be made by a borrower (present value), expressed as a percentage of the loan's face value. Source: International Monetary Fund https://www.imf.org/external/np/spr/2015/conc/index.htm#:~:text=The%20degree%20of%20concessionality%20of,percentage%20of%20the%20loan's%20face (retrieved in October 2020).

[8] Ministry of Finance of Georgia, Statistical Bulletin of Public Debt of Georgia N1, December 2013. https://mof.ge/images/File/debt-bulletin/Public-Sector-Debt-Statistical-Bulletin-N1_GEO-Final.pdf (retrieved in October 2020).

capital markets and where the boundary between domestic and external public debt is less pronounced. Because the weighted average interest rate on Georgia's public external debt stock was less than 2%, a switch from the concessional long-term public external debt to the shorter-term public domestic debt was not rushed. Currency stability mitigated exchange rate risks.

An increase in GDP per capita decreases eligibility for concessional forms of external public borrowing. This might increase Georgia's reliance on the domestic public borrowing. This may (1) support de-dollarization and mitigate exchange rate risks; (2) enhance commercial banks' liquidity management toolkit as treasuries are pledged as collateral with central bank for liquidity management purposes; (3) help to price corporate risks and to develop domestic commercial tradable debt; (4) support the mandatory second pillar of a pension system by broadening domestic investment opportunities; and (5) facilitate management of monetary aggregates and inflation targeting.

Access to International Capital Markets

By the end of 2012, sovereign Eurobonds represented one-tenth of Georgia's public debt. Why did Georgia issue its first Eurobond in 2008 and then refinance it in 2011, given its access to the concessional international assistance? In general, why would a sovereign issue a Eurobond without an immediate financing need? Can such Eurobond promote private investment?

In April of 2008, to promote its reputation, Georgia was the first country in the Caucasus to issue a US$ 500 million five-year debut Eurobond. It was more than three times oversubscribed and priced at 7.5%—the tight end of the market. In April of 2011, Georgia issued a ten-year Eurobond and used proceeds to redeem the previous bond through an "any and all" cash tender. Priced at the lower yield of 7.125%, the 2011 Eurobond broadened the investor base (RegS/144A in 2011 versus RegS in 2008), increased liquidity and established a longer sovereign benchmark.

The landmark status of these two transactions anchored Georgia to investors' radars and established an independent yardstick for measurement of its sovereign risk. It fostered non-sovereign issuances from Georgia. Subsequent Eurobond issuances by the Georgian Railways, Georgian Oil and Gas Corporation and commercial banks were helped by

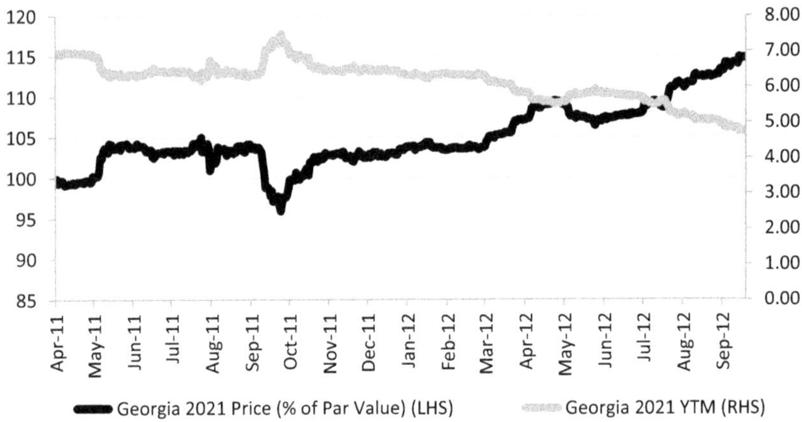

Fig. 13.3 Georgia's 2011 Eurobond, secondary market performance from issuance till end- September 2012 (*Source* Ministry of Finance of Georgia)[9]

a good secondary market performance of Georgia's sovereign Eurobond (Fig. 13.3) whose yield to maturity compared favorably to yields for sovereigns in the same credit rating category.

More than three hundred international investors invested in Georgia's debt and equity securities—the rather unprecedented breadth of the investor coverage for a small economy. Prior to the 2008 Eurobond, an aggregate volume of non-sovereign Eurobond issuances from Georgia was approximately US$ 200 million. It increased thereafter.

Decisions to issue Eurobonds in 2008 and 2011 in the absence of an immediate need to borrow were linked to two questions: how to measure Georgia's sovereign creditworthiness and to impose scrutiny on the government's performance? How to anchor Georgia to radars of investors?

A secondary market performance of a Eurobond reflects investors' view on an issuing sovereign. Investors study the sovereign because they have their money at stake. The secondary market performance thus reflects a market perception of an issuing sovereign. It guides potential foreign

[9] YTM is yield to maturity, expressed in percent. YTM is a discount rate which makes present value of all future cash flows of a bond (coupon payments, repayment of principal at maturity) equal to the bond's market price. The higher the bond yield, the lower the market price of a bond and vice versa. Risky bonds trade at higher yields and lower prices.

direct and portfolio investors into its real and financial sectors. Such international scrutiny rewards reformers, punishes laggards and thus creates performance incentives.

Two main questions are: is an issuing sovereign able and willing to work with investors into its Eurobond to prompt them into exploring non-sovereign opportunities within the same country? Can domestic banks and firms benefit from a benchmark established by a sovereign Eurobond to tap international debt and equity markets?

Georgia sought to transform itself into a multi-sectoral regional platform for services and manufacturing, spearheaded by international investment. From 2009, the "regional hub economy" vision moved to the center of Georgia's economic positioning. Relations with sovereign Eurobonds' investors thus mattered beyond the immediate cash. Such relationship must be maintained through an economic performance, political stability and banks' and firms' ability to use it for their benefit. Unless this holds, the case for issuing sovereign Eurobonds without an immediate borrowing need weakens.

International Assistance

In 2004–2012, Georgia benefited from cooperation with international development partners. In public sector, it materialized, *inter alia*, through infrastructure finance and budget support. In private sector, through credit lines through commercial banks and through direct support of bankable projects in the real sector.

Georgia's aid dependency decreased in 2004–2008 until the global financial crisis and the war with Russia in 2008. In October 2008, the European Union and the United States co-sponsored a donor conference which pledged US$ 4 billion to close Georgia's fiscal gap in 2008–2009, support internally displaced persons and develop infrastructure. In four years, this pledge was converted into contractual commitments. Representatives of multilateral development banks confided that implementation of infrastructure projects in Georgia was faster than anything they had seen before.

Key factors in the context of the management of international assistance in Georgia were:

- **Strong mandate of the Ministry of Finance (MOF)**, which ensured a proper interface between foreign aid, public debt and budget management. MOF negotiated all public sector loans and grants which were reflected in the budget or had material policy implications. MOF was responsible for timely disbursement of reforms-based budget support where breach of conditionalities could trigger disbursement delays. Disbursement rates under such budget support schemes were close to 100%. Where ministries of finance dodge this responsibility, development partners negotiate with multiple counterparts: ministries of economy which draft development strategies, advisors to prime ministers and line ministers who pursue their own goals, and are less aware of public debt affordability constraints. An ensuing maze of decision-making does not help.

- **Coordination set-up.** Complaints on lack of donor coordination are not uncommon, although pragmatic discussions on the topic are sometimes missing. Large development partners try to coordinate among each other and with host governments because their support (loans in the first place) is reflected in budgets and in public debt. This does not preclude their competition for projects because, for example, multilateral development banks' performance scorecards include business volumes in countries of operation. Then, there are smaller development partners providing off-budget grants, technical assistance and capacity building. Embassies managing development cooperation budgets are tempted to stretch them across sectors to enhance visibility. Some bilateral donors tie their aid to own consultants and equipment. Development partners pursue multi-year planning which reflects priorities in their capitals and at their headquarters. This influences their margins of manoeuver.

Bearing in mind this complexity, Georgia's message was threefold: (1) donor coordination is a joint responsibility; (2) MOF handles assistance which has material financial and policy-related implications and is reflected in budget; (3) line ministries handle sectoral assistance directly, provided that important commitments must be aligned with national priorities. Such "concentric circles" vision bestowed upon MOF the key role in coordinating "big ticket" items and devolved to other public entities the responsibility for sectoral donor coordination.

- **Strong project implementation units.** The Roads Department was strengthened to accelerate preparation and implementation of projects without compromising on quality. To consolidate management of municipal projects, the government established the Municipal Development Fund. This benefitted sectors where international assistance was significant. Vigilance of law enforcement agencies mitigated corruption risks. Sound project cycle management reduced price escalation risks (amounts of infrastructure loans negotiated with development finance institutions are often based on feasibility studies, whereas detailed project designs are funded from loan proceeds after loan agreements are signed; this might lead to cost overruns).
- **National ownership.** Policy reform matrices agreed with development partners have limits. Too many matrices increase paperwork without triggering big changes. Even the International Monetary Fund which has the largest leverage in times of crises may get bogged down in governance conditionalities stretching beyond monetary, fiscal and exchange rate policies. Policy reform matrices can help, but a heavy lifting must be done by national leaders.
- **No "parallel structures."** Pinning hope on new "parallel structures" when core institutions (e.g., core institutions which fight corruption, etc.) malfunction is akin to stopping a train with a sermon. Developing countries' politics often outlives pubic institutions. A political consensus which drives international development partners' belief in a "parallel" institutional breakthrough can unravel with next elections. "Parallel structures" may provide smokescreens behind which corrupt and mismanaged core institutions continue as usual and eventually put the "parallel structures" into choke hold. If there is no will to transform core institutions, expect tricks to subvert the new "parallel structures." All along, national leaders speaking at international conferences praise the "parallel structures" as big achievements.
- **Simplicity.** Complex projects over-spend on administration and monitoring. Beneficiaries receive less as a result. MOF sought to minimize the complexity of public sector projects.

CHAPTER 14

Wealth Generation, Taxes, Customs, Trade and Logistics

Abstract This chapter explains the wealth creation process. It discusses Georgia's tax liberalization reforms and political and economic factors which allowed it to succeed. It explains Georgia's customs, tariff and trade liberalization and how it supported Georgia's regional economic positioning.

Keywords Wealth · Tax · Customs · Trade · Logistics · Regional hub · Transportation

Who Creates Wealth?

No developing country has leapfrogged without an efficient and visionary government. But wealth is created mainly by private citizens who spot opportunities, generate ideas, borrow, put at stake own money, outmaneuver competitors, address threats from new entrants, strike deals with suppliers and buyers, defend market position and handle government regulations.[1] All this to generate revenue to recover costs, repay loans, pay taxes and retain profit, thus *adding value*.

[1] See Porter (2008) on Five Forces framework which analyses a company's competitive environment.

D. Gvindadze, *The Transformation of Georgia from 2004 to 2012*,
https://doi.org/10.1007/978-3-031-18264-8_14

Some entrepreneurs become rich; others go bankrupt. Where governments are corrupt or inefficient, entrepreneurs add value *despite*—rather than *thanks to*—their governments. A gross domestic product (GDP) of a country is an annual sum of values added by such entrepreneurs through their skin-in-the-game decisions. A sustained GDP growth enhances a stock of national wealth. Tax revenues increase and governments provide better social safety, infrastructure and national security.

Governments which understand this causality launch their countries on paths of growth. Governments which misread it become bloated and counterproductive. They misinterpret market failures and misallocate resources. Their fiscal and monetary stimulus measures fail due to productive constraints in economies, because intended boosts to a domestic demand translate into a deterioration in net exports. They attract too many people into the relative safety of public sector jobs. Such jobs limit downside risks, restrict the upside and thus mainstream a cap-and-collar mentality inhibiting the entrepreneurship and the wealth creation. Public bureaucracies become a burden for a shrinking pool of entrepreneurs. When this happens, outcomes are painful: stagnation, abrupt economic adjustments, debased currencies, social and political distress, bailouts, bail-ins, unemployment and poverty.

In this chapter and Chapter 15 I explain the transformation of Georgia's business climate in 2004–2012.

Tax Reform—More Than a Reduction in Taxes

From 2004, Georgia's tax policy and administration underwent a major transformation.[2]

- The number of taxes—21 before 2004[3]—was reduced to 7 from 2005 and to 6 from 2008 (Table 14.1). Taxation became flat: same tax rate applied across income brackets. Progressive taxation ended amid understanding that it would unleash race to the bottom where

[2] Georgia Pocket Tax Book (2012).

[3] State taxes: income tax, profit tax, VAT, excise, property tax, social insurance tax, property transfer tax, vehicle tax, natural resource tax, environment tax, tax on transport entry on the territory and overload tax, flat tax, small business tax. Local taxes: tax for business activities, gambling tax, recreational tax, hotel tax, advertisement tax, tax for using local symbols, land tax, parking tax. Source: N. Gilauri (2017).

lawyers representing individuals and firms in top income brackets would work to decrease tax burden on their clients. Such race to the bottom is a particular challenge in developing countries seeking income equality at the expense of simplicity and efficiency and end up with neither.

- Loopholes and tax avoidance schemes were closed through carrots (streamlined policies, digitalized and modernized administration, as explained below) and sticks (prosecution of economic crime and corruption). Improved tax code reduced risks of a dual interpretation of its provisions. This work benefitted from a two-tier tax dispute resolution board at the Ministry of Finance which together with tax specialists of the ministry included independent experts and representatives of audit firms.
- Aversion to protectionism and to the industrial policy meant that no special interest groups could claim a preferential tax treatment for sectors and companies.
- Tax rates were reduced. VAT decreased from 20% in 2004 to 18% from 2006. Personal income tax (12–20% in 2004) became flat 12% in 2005. After abolishment of the social tax (33% in 2004 and 20% in 2005–2007), personal income tax became 25% in 2008 and 20% from 2009 (all social payments were paid from a general budget revenue pool). Corporate income tax was reduced from 20% in 2004 to 15% from 2008. Dividend and interest income tax was reduced from 10% in 2004 to 5% from 2009. The authorities committed to a further gradual decrease across tax rates.
- Fiscally insignificant and "special" taxes were scrapped to avoid red tape and to minimize tax evasion. Georgia emerged with no payroll or social insurance tax, no capital gains tax, no wealth tax, no inheritance tax or stamp duty, no property transfer tax. Foreign source income of individuals is tax exempt. Dividend on free floating debt and equity securities and interest paid by licensed financial institutions became tax exempt. Companies re-exporting foreign goods through Georgia paid no profit tax, VAT and import tax. Financial institutions whose Georgia-sourced income did not exceed 10% of their global income became eligible for a status of an international financial company which exempted them from a profit tax, dividend and interest tax and VAT. Hotels with a special status in free tourist zones became exempt from a corporate income tax and property tax. Simplified accounting and taxation applied to micro-

and small businesses. The government created several free economic zones, but their impact was marginal. The goal was to modernize the entire country rather than creating niches of efficiency in a sea of a red tape.

- All national taxes accrued to the central budget. Only a property tax of up to 1% of property value is a local tax. Households above an annual income threshold pay it, applying a tax coefficient to a self-assessed value of a real estate they own. Centralized revenue collection meant moderate fiscal decentralization to retain leverage over budget allocation.
- Georgia emerged from the tax reform with no sectoral taxes and no sectoral tax revenue earmarks. Tax revenues were allocated to spending units annually from the general budget. This enhanced the budget's agility and averted creation of special funds accumulating and spending sectoral tax revenues. For example, instead of a road usage tax accruing to a road maintenance fund, Georgia's Roads Department (part of the Ministry of Regional Development and Infrastructure) and municipalities were receiving annual allocations for construction and maintenance of roads from the central budget.

Having simplified its tax policy, Georgia sought to preclude future policy reversals. In July 2011, the Parliament adopted an organic law on economic freedom (Liberty Act) which obliged the government to submit to a referendum any introduction of new national taxes (except excise) or any increase of existing tax rates (except when a new tax replaces an existing national tax without increasing a tax burden). The referendum could not be sought to introduce progressive taxation. Given aversion to high taxes and its likely impact on an outcome of a referendum, these provisions meant that a permanent tax increase could only materialize in special circumstances (this does not mean that a government with a different economic thinking cannot unravel the Liberty Act; reversions to the mean happen).

A political consensus behind the tax liberalization of 2004–2012 mitigated risks of a blame game in case of unexpected tax revenue outcomes. The tax policy liberalization broadened the tax base and increased tax revenues. The latter was helped by other aspects of Georgia's transformation from 2004:

- Fast growth through liberalization of trade, deregulation and modernization of public services, simplification of labor legislation, privatization and corporatization of state-owned enterprises, investments, anti-crime and anti-corruption policies and economic stability.
- Modernization of the tax and customs administration to close tax avoidance schemes, cut middlemen, replace personnel, improve processes, consolidate databases, mainstream risk-based audits, e-solutions and service orientation, roll out on-demand services, modernize infrastructure and by 2011–2012 rebrand Georgia's Revenue Service to emphasize openness and accessibility.

The strategy paid off. The ratio of total annual tax and customs revenues to GDP increased from 14% in 2003 to approximately 26% in 2007 and then stabilized at approximately 25% of GDP (Fig. 14.1). Tax revenues increased from GEL 1228.6 million in 2003 to GEL 6671 million in 2012, an almost 5.5-fold increase translating into a compound annual growth rate (CAGR) of 20% (note that in 2004–2012 average annual consumer price inflation was at a single digit level). General government expenditure increased from approximately 16.5% of GDP in 2003 to 30% in 2007 and thereafter, with capital spending representing as much as one-quarter of such expenditure. In 2012, Georgia's total tax rate in percent of commercial profits was the lowest in the region.

What's next for Georgia's tax system? UNCTAD's 2020 World Investment Report explains impact of the COVID-19 crisis from 2020 on global foreign direct investment (FDI). The crisis hit investment in greenfield projects, cross-border mergers and acquisitions and global project finance which funnels FDI to infrastructure projects. It multiplied existing trade, financial and geopolitical tensions. FDI to transition economies in Europe is hit, FDI recovery is uncertain and competition for FDI is

Table 14.1 Georgia's tax liberalization timeline

	2004	2005	2006	2007	2008	2009	2010	2011	2012
Number of taxes	21 ↓	7	7	7 ↓	6	6	6	6	6
VAT	20%	20% ↓	18%	18%	18%	18%	18%	18%	18%
Personal income tax	12%-20% ↓	12%	12%	12%	Soc+pers.inc. tax 32% ↓ 25%	Soc+pers.inc. tax ↓ 20%	20%	20%	20%
Social tax	33% ↓	20%	20%	20%	n/a	n/a	n/a	n/a	n/a
Corporate income tax	20%	20%	20%	20% ↓	15%	15%	15%	15%	15%
Dividend and interest income tax	10%	10%	10%	10%	10% ↓	5%	5%	5%	5%

Source Ministry of Finance of Georgia

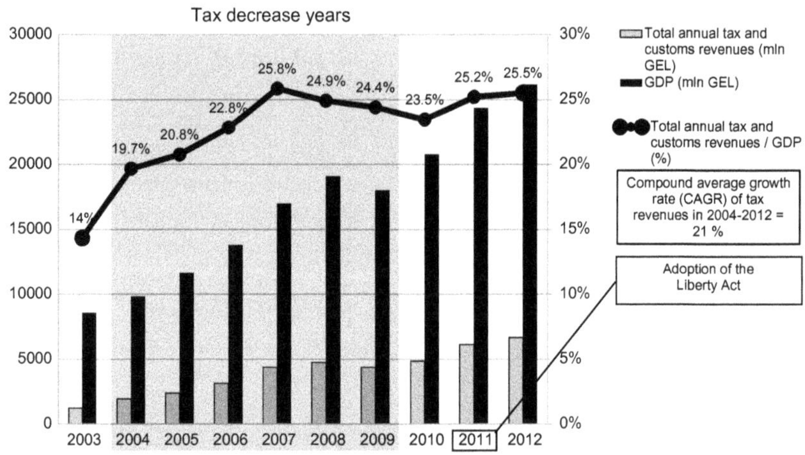

Fig. 14.1 Impact of the tax liberalization on the government revenues in Georgia, 2003–2012 (*Source* Ministry of Finance of Georgia)

expected to rise.[4] In this context, a broad-brush forward-thinking on the taxation might be as follows:

- **Continuous tax liberalization.** GDP is the sum of a value added by domestic firms. Absent tax loopholes, revenue from Georgia's 18% VAT would roughly translate into the VAT tax revenue to GDP ratio of up to 18%. Together with revenue from property tax (income based, to protect poor households which own or inherit a real estate) and excise tax (levied on goods and services with negative environmental and health externalities), this translates into a total tax revenue to GDP ratio of more than 20%. Imagine a head of state announcing annually that personal and/or corporate income tax rates would decrease by up to 1% (subject to the global agreement on corporate taxation in case of profit tax).[5] The personal and

[4] International Production Beyond Pandemic, World Investment Report 2020, United Nations Conference on Trade and Development https://unctad.org/system/files/official-document/wir2020_en.pdf.

[5] An impact of the corporate tax rate reduction on competitiveness depends on the global corporate tax reform discussion at G7, G20 and OECD, of which imposition of a minimum global corporate tax rate is part.

corporate income taxes can be reduced gradually and the VAT rate can be adjusted to accommodate spending priorities. The message to the private sector might be powerful. It can reinforce Georgia's liberal credentials (when many other countries are adrift) and force the government into thinking of what else to outsource to the private sector through privatization or public–private partnerships, how to expand modern and financially self-sustainable public services and how to improve quality of spending. The feasibility of this approach depends on Georgia's *social contract*. This approach is the polar opposite of creating new spending lines and then hiking taxes or hardening tax administration to fund them. Singapore, for example, developed with government revenues and expenditures not exceeding 20% of GDP (Fig. 14.2).

- **Reimagining the tax authority**. Technology can revolutionize tax collection and interaction between individuals and the state. It can allow to collect taxes in real time, to reduce evasion and increase fairness. Real-time tax reporting driven by personalized data on incomes and expenditures can help calibrate the social safety net in a way which rewards the neediest, thus resulting in spending-side efficiencies.[6] Cost- corruption- and bureaucracy-reduction effects of a real-time paperwork-free taxation and of calibrated social safety nets might seem far-fetched, but implications are significant. McKinsey & Company reimagines tax authorities for the digital future where accountants are replaced with a cloud-based accounting software and where fintech and instant account-to-account payments become ubiquitous. A tax authority reinvented for such future would prioritize (1) full digitization and integration into the network of transactions and payments, which entails a shift from the legacy operating model to a consumer-facing technology company; (2) innovative talent management to integrate technologists and data experts; (3) a citizen-centric culture to build trust as interaction with taxpayers becomes less visible but more real time and ubiquitous.[7]

[6] Expect the taxman of the future to take your money in real time. *Financial Times*, 5 November 2019.

[7] Reimagining Tax Authorities for the Future (16 October 2020), McKinsey & Company. https://www.mckinsey.com/industries/public-and-social-sector/our-insights/reimagining-tax-authorities-for-the-future.

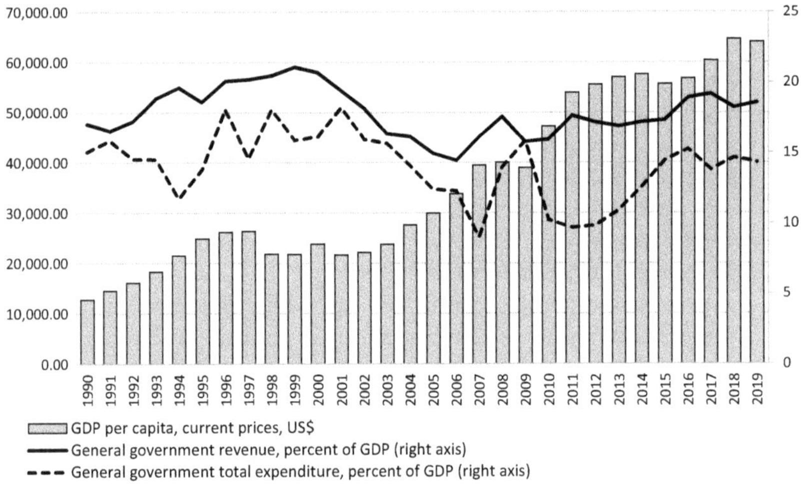

Fig. 14.2 Singapore's GDP per capita and size of the government in 1990–2019 (*Source* International Memory Fund. World Economic Outlook Database [October 2019])

Customs, Trade and Transportation

Customs and trade legislation which Georgia inherited in 2004 dated back to the 1990s. It triggered an average tariff in excess of 20% (16 tariffs from zero to 30%). Non-tariff barriers to trade and their enforcement by several agencies led to corruption. Collection of customs revenues at ports of entry (as opposed to an inland collection) congested clearance procedures and trade. Incentives for bribery and mis-reporting were rampant.

From 2004, Georgia unilaterally liberalized its trade regime and streamlined public services (Fig. 14.3). Around 90% of imports to Georgia qualified under zero tariff rate. Rates of 5 and 12% applied to certain goods in sensitive domestic market segments. Georgia reported such zero tariffs to the World Trade Organization (WTO) as bound tariff rates to prevent future revisions of the tariff policy. The new norms applied to all countries, irrespective of their WTO membership (Georgia is the WTO member since 2000). Strong bias against protectionism,

In 2005-2012, the number of documents to export decreased from 9 to 4; the number of documents to import decreased from 15 to 4.

In 2012, Georgia's simple mean applied tariff* (all products) was fifth lowest globaly (after Singapore, Macao SAR, Hong Kong SAR and Norway), out of all countries for which data for a given year was reported. Georgia's weighted mean tariff ** was also fifth lowest globally (after Singapore, Macao SAR, Hong Kong SAR and Norway), out of all countries for which data for a given year was reported.

* Simple mean applied tariff is the unweighted average of effectively applied rates for all products subject to tariffs calculated for all traded goods.

** Weighted mean applied tariff is the average of effectively applied rates weighted by the product import shares corresponding to each partner country.

Source: The World Bank *(The World Bank's estimates using the World Integrated Trade Solution system, based on UNCTAD's and WTOs databases)*

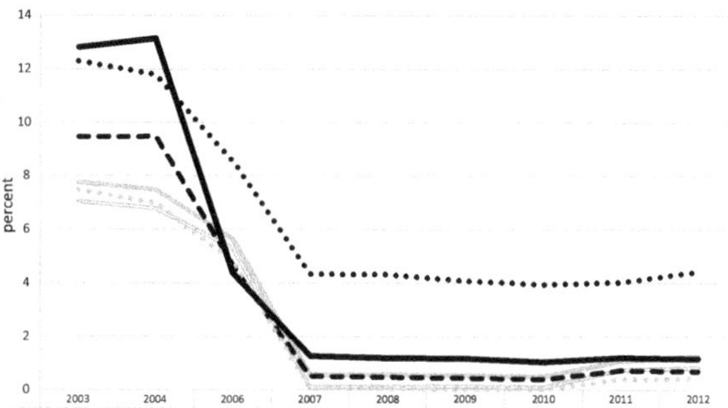

	2003	2004	2006	2007	2008	2009	2010	2011	2012
Tariff rate, applied, simple mean, all products (%)	7.75	7.49	5.64	0.57	0.57	0.54	0.5	1.07	1.25
Tariff rate, applied, simple mean, manufactured products (%)	7.04	6.78	5.29	0.11	0.11	0.12	0.09	0.74	0.82
Tariff rate, applied, simple mean, primary products (%)	12.3	11.8	8.55	4.34	4.32	4.08	3.95	4.03	4.43
Tariff rate, applied, weighted mean, all products (%)	9.47	9.48	4.65	0.5	0.47	0.43	0.39	0.72	0.68
Tariff rate, applied, weighted mean, manufactured products (%)	7.48	6.99	4.82	0.06	0.06	0.02	0.02	0.4	0.42
Tariff rate, applied, weighted mean, primary products (%)	12.82	13.15	4.36	1.26	1.18	1.16	1.04	1.19	1.14

Fig. 14.3 Georgia's tariff liberalization path (2003–2012)

absence of technical non-tariff barriers to trade and of quotas, voluntary product standards (except in public health and safety areas) and zero tariffs on export, re-export and transit fostered trade diversification and increased volumes.[8]

Transformation of Georgia's customs administration in 2004–2012 can be split into the same stages as of the tax administration, with initial heavy-handed approach to uproot crime followed by an institutional modernization. Customs infrastructure was fully rebuilt. Roads to main customs checkpoints were repaired. New checkpoints were opened or re-opened in areas where cross-border exchanges could ignite additional regional growth. Working conditions improved. Old offices were replaced with open spaces in modern glass buildings. Simple processes and consolidated databases eliminated red tape and cut off middlemen. Dozens of customs officers were caught red-handed, fired or imprisoned. Their replacements had no record of serving in the customs administration when it had been notoriously corrupt. Risk management modules and automation soon minimized discretion of customs officers, cut paperwork and ensured a faster impartial treatment.[9] Companies with a good record of compliance with customs procedures and posing no evasion

[8] L. Gurgenidze (2009).

[9] N. Beruashvili, O. McGill (2010).

or smuggling-related risks were included in the Golden List. It simplified customs treatment, including post-clearance payment of customs fees. The number of public entities operating customs checkpoints decreased from nine to two: Patrol Police of the Ministry of Interior and the Revenue Service of the Ministry of Finance. Transformation of the Patrol Police happened earlier than in the customs administration, due to its specificity and the political weight of the Ministry of Interior. Such joint effort by the two entities helped the Revenue Service. To have their documents processed, drivers no longer needed to exit cars.

In 2010, Georgia pioneered Customs Clearance Zones (CCZ). Imported cargo started being fast-tracked through checkpoints and forwarded to related CCZs providing comprehensive single window services. Importers filing advance declarations could have their documents processed even at their final destination. Crossing borders became fast and easy. Trade turnover increased significantly on the back of high growth and enhanced customs throughput capacity (Fig. 14.4). From 2014, Georgia's free trade network was boosted by the Deep and Comprehensive Free Trade Agreement with the European Union.

Economic openness, modern tax and customs administrations and corruption-free public services (including services by the Service Agency of the Ministry of Interior) transformed Georgia into a regional hub for trading of motor cars. By 2012, Georgia's exports of motor cars represented 25% of its total export, up from zero in 2003. Companies and individuals started bringing to Georgia new and used cars to sell them mainly in the Caucasus and in Central Asia. This created thousands of jobs in parking, auto repair and other auxiliary services. It offered the example of how Georgia could leverage its transit function in other areas.

To enhance its transshipment orientation (by 2012, transshipment values amounted to three times Georgia's GDP) and its logistical potential, Georgia abolished transit barriers, fees and quotas, commercialized railway tariffs and liberalized its international aviation market. Georgia became better accessible, with travelers free to choose among transportation options.

Heritage Foundation's 2013 Index of Economic Freedom (based on data from the second half of 2011 through the first half of 2012) ranked Georgia seventh out of 180 countries in its "trade freedom" measure (a

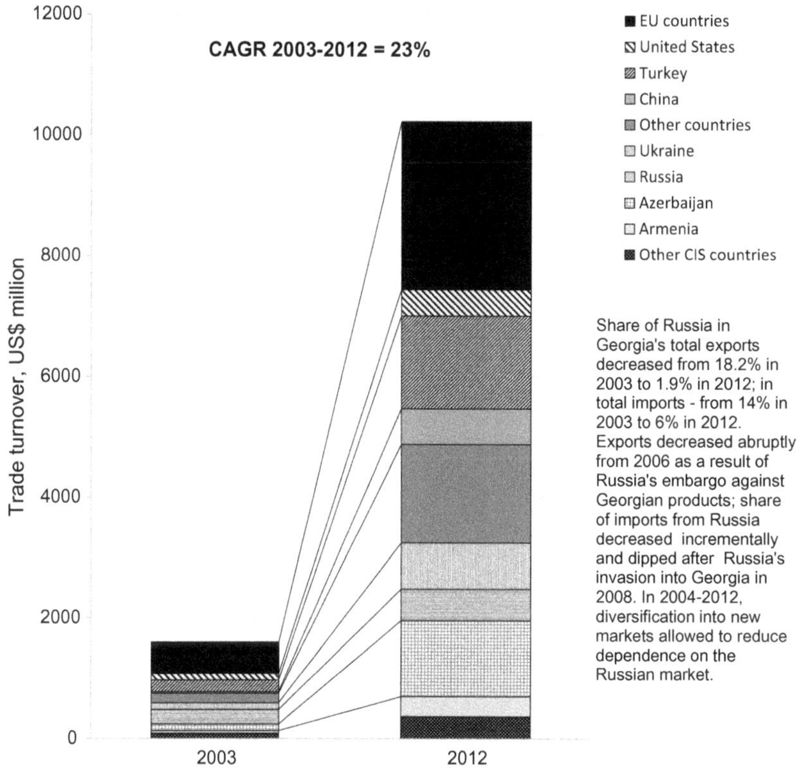

Fig. 14.4 Increase in Georgia's trade turnover, 2003 and 2012 (*Source* Geostat)

composite measure of the absence of tariff and non-tariff barriers that affect imports and exports of goods and services). Georgia's degree of trade freedom exceeded that of any of its main trade partners in 2004–2012.

CHAPTER 15

De-regulation, Privatization, Public Services and Competition

Abstract This chapter discusses Georgia's improved business climate, modernized public services, regulatory simplification and outsourcing, liberalized labor regulations, equal treatment of foreign and domestic investors, privatization and corporatization of state-owned enterprises and assets, liberalized visa and residence permit rules, competition and economic freedom.

Keywords Public services · Regulation · Privatization · Visa · Business climate · Competition

In 2004, Georgia's GDP per capita was approximately US$ 1000. The country ranked low in the World Bank's Doing Business ranking and was classified as a "mostly unfree" economy in the Index of Economic Freedom of the Heritage Foundation, largely due to cumbersome regulations.

Modernization of agencies delivering public services which gained pace after 2004 removed bureaucracy which was both feeding and fed by an excessive regulation. It targeted entities handling permits, registrations and licenses (ministries, civil and public registries, municipalities, etc.). Public entities which failed the test of relevance were downsized or

D. Gvindadze, *The Transformation of Georgia from 2004 to 2012*,
https://doi.org/10.1007/978-3-031-18264-8_15

dismantled. Those whose mandate was relevant yet the ability to fulfill it was absent were reengineered.[1]

In Georgia's closely knit society where everyone is everyone's neighbor, friend or relative, the optimization on this scale was difficult. Still, the government repealed approximately 70% and 90% of some 300 licenses and 600 permits.[2] It halved the number of inspection agencies. A new law in 2005 minimized the number of licenses, specified activities requiring licenses and permits and clarified procedures.

The government realized that a strong regulatory capacity would take time to develop and that over-reliance on domestic standards and codes would add red tape or uncertainty without producing best outcomes. So it applied the "regulatory outsourcing" whereby technical standards and codes of advanced economies were treated on par with national standards. Georgia abolished re-licensing for pharmaceuticals licensed in advanced economies. Technical standards and codes of the European Union and the Organisation for Economic Cooperation and Development (OECD) were allowed to be used alongside national norms. Imported consumer goods, including processed food, certified in the OECD countries required no re-certification.[3] The regulatory outsourcing increased domestic competition by facilitating entries by new market participants and enabling them to compete on pricing and client acquisition strategies.

From 2005, public agencies started providing licenses, certificates and permits through their one-stop-shops ("single windows"). The "silence is consent" principle set deadlines for replying to citizens' requests. Upon expiry of such deadlines, licenses, certificates and permits were considered granted. This changed behavior of civil servants because breach of deadlines entailed loss of control over decisions and personal career risks. Georgia then consolidated the "single window" services into twelve "Public Service Halls" (PSH) built in 2011–2012 in all main cities. Serving more than 16,000 customers daily, PSHs integrated under one roof more than 300 services. They proposed transactional and operational improvements which set a new international standard of public service innovation.[4] PHSs' customer spaces feature consolidated front

[1] Fighting Corruption in Public Services: Chronicling Georgia's Reforms (2012).

[2] Georgian Reform—Success Stories (2009).

[3] L. Gurgenidze (2009).

[4] Public Service Hall home page (www.psh.gov.ge).

desks representing ministries and public agencies. Front-officers work with middle and back offices. A "one government" approach meant that a customer could not be asked by one public entity to bring a certificate from another public entity. A new service culture which thus emerged was discussed for replication in other countries.

A new labor code in 2006 devolved to employers and employees much of the responsibility for agreeing contractual terms, including working days per week, overtime work and remuneration package (no minimum wage requirements). Indefinitely renewable fixed-term contracts of any duration were allowed for permanent tasks. Notice period for the redundancy dismissal was set at zero and the severance pay was equalized to a one-month salary, irrespective of a worker's tenure.[5] Collective bargaining was allowed by any group rather than by trade unions alone. Same set of rules and principles applied to nationals and non-citizens. Foreign nationals were allowed to obtain formal employment without work permits. Such contractual relationship—once established—became sufficient to receive residency. In the 2013 Index of Economic Freedom of the Heritage Foundation (data of 2009–2012), Georgia's labor freedom score was third highest globally, behind the United States and Singapore.

Foreign and domestic investors received equal treatment in respect of land, ownership rights, repatriation of assets and funds. Land and other immovable assets could be bought and sold freely. The state set no tariffs for private companies, except in relation to natural monopolies.

In 2004–2012, Georgia privatized many state-owned assets. Simple deals were the priority. The privatization also involved deals where upfront prices paid by investors reflected their future obligations regarding purchased assets. The process was helped by Georgia's positive international image, anti-corruption and anti-crime measures. The political consolidation fostered fast decisions. Where these conditions are absent: (1) investors do not come, so loss-making assets and enterprises rust in public ownership or (2) a privatization becomes a smokescreen for asset-strippers and those who wish to legalize their de facto control over state assets.

By 2012, the state owned a limited number of strategic enterprises, including the Georgian Railways (Georgia's integrated rail company

[5] Doing Business (2013).

whose business mainly stems from Georgia's location as the shortest transportation route from the Black Sea to the Caspian Sea), Georgian Oil and Gas Corporation (ensures security of gas supply to Georgia and represents the state in international energy transit projects) and Georgian State Electrosystem (provides in-country and cross-border high voltage electricity transmission and exclusive dispatch services). Both Georgian Railways and the Georgian Oil and Gas Corporation issued Eurobonds to fund their development. In 2012, the government thought of listing of the Georgian Railways' small stake on the London Stock Exchange (this did not materialize due to market conditions).

Unreformed state-owned enterprises (SOEs) produce risks. Shares' listing might enhance scrutiny and reduce pressures to which SOEs are exposed. If SOE production target setting is political, then shareholder value maximization becomes secondary to employment and output. Tariffs might not reflect costs and externalities. Risks of misprocurement, favoritism and toxic interlocking exposures with banks increase. SOEs-led industrialization policies when a government picks "growth champions" might mobilize FDI and increase sectoral outputs, but this might happen at the expense of other sectors and at a high opportunity cost. Such "growth champions" might fail to become competitive and enhance exports, despite high fiscal costs. SOEs receiving a subsidized state funding get addicted to it. This reduces incentive for corporate bond issuance and other commercial forms of financing which require credit quality appraisals.

Georgia largely unilaterally liberalized visa and residence permit rules for foreign citizens. In 2012, citizens of more than 90 countries—including from the EU and the OECD—did not need a visa to enter and stay in Georgia for a year. Visa-free regime applied to almost all countries of the Commonwealth of Independent States. Russia's citizens could enter Georgia visa-free and stay for up to three months, despite the absence of diplomatic relations. Visas up to one year could be issued at border crossing points. Foreign nationals in possession of valid multiple-entry visas of the EU and the Schengen countries and of the United States could enter Georgia visa-free and stay up to three months, provided that their mentioned multiple-entry visas remained valid and that they had been used at least once. Visa extension rules and procedures of issuing temporary or permanent residence permits were simplified. No administrative sanction applied if delays in leaving Georgia did not exceed 10 days. Longer delays triggered a fine payable before or after exiting the country.

This—together with the improved personal safety, the "open skies" policy, international promotion of Georgia, development of a hospitality infrastructure, enhanced international and domestic connectivity and a broadened offering across attractions and services—increased the number of international arrivals in Georgia from 310,000 in 2003 to 4,389,000 in 2012 (an almost 14-fold increase implying a compound annual growth rate of 34%). The World Bank Development Indicators database attributed Georgia to the global top-five of the fastest growing international tourism destinations (international inbound tourists, 2003–2011). Georgia's international tourism receipts as a percentage of total exports of goods and services increased from 14% in 2003 to 26% in 2012.

In the World Bank's Doing Business (DB) indicators, Georgia improved its rank from 137th out of 183 countries in 2004 to 9th out of 185 countries in 2013 (DB-2013 data is current as of 1 June 2012; ahead of Georgia in the DB-2013 ranking were Singapore, Hong Kong SAR China, New Zealand, United States, Denmark, Norway, United Kingdom and Republic of Korea). In 2005–2012, Georgia progressed more than any other country in narrowing its "distance to the frontier" (the distance to frontier shows how far an economy is from the best performance achieved by any economy on each DB indicator since 2005).[6] Georgia's reforms across DB indicators were among the most ambitious globally.

In 2004–2012, Georgia progressed from 79th to 21st global rank in the Heritage Foundation's Index of Economic Freedom. In the 2013

[6] For the 2004 Doing Business rank, see World Bank Country Economic Memorandum "Georgia Rising: Sustaining Rapid Economic Growth," July 2013. For the 2013 rank and distance to the frontier, see World Bank. 2013. Doing Business 2013: Smarter Regulations for Small and Medium-Size Enterprises. The 2013 Ease of Doing Business rank reflected counties' performance along ten indicators: starting a business, dealing with construction permits, getting electricity, registering property, getting credit, protecting investors, paying taxes, trading across borders, enforcing contracts, resolving insolvency. Note that the World Bank discontinued the Doing Business report in September 2021.

Index of Economic Freedom (based on data from the second half of 2011 through the first half of 2012), Georgia ranked higher than Central and Eastern European countries (except Estonia which ranked 13th). Georgia was upgraded from the "*mostly unfree*" to the "*mostly free*" category.[7]

According to the World Governance Indicators, the improvement in the "regulatory quality" estimate (reflects perception of the ability of the government to formulate and implement sound policies and regulations that permit and promote private sector development) in Georgia in 2004–2012 was the highest *globally*.[8]

In 2004–2012, Georgia had no anti-monopoly agency. A relationship between such agencies and market competition in developing economies is complex. Anti-monopoly work requires a deep understanding of firms-level and sectoral trends. Where such understanding is lacking and a political economy is not conducive, anti-monopoly agencies risk becoming verdict-trading law enforcement units. A narrow fixation on these agencies can deflect attention from the regulatory liberalization, institutional optimization and fight against crime and corruption. Solid anti-monopoly agencies can add value, but competition in developing countries is best promoted through an economic freedom.

Monopolies in developing countries mirror domestic politics. Think of a businessman fronting for a public official and monopolizing import of fuel or cereals, or of a minister of energy who is a significant energy sector investor, or of a central bank governor holding hidden stakes in commercial banks. The challenge here is not technical. It is unlikely to be resolved by an anti-monopoly agency, especially if it reports to a council chaired by officials behind the monopolies.

[7] 2013 Index of Economic Freedom, the Heritage Foundation and Dow Jones & Company, Inc. The Index of Economic Freedom covers 10 freedoms: property rights, freedom from corruption, fiscal freedom, government spending, business freedom, labor freedom, monetary freedom, trade freedom, investment freedom, financial freedom. A country's overall economic freedom score is a simple average of its scores on the 10 individual freedoms.

[8] World Bank, World Governance Indicators.

CHAPTER 16

Banking

Abstract This chapter explains Georgia's banking sector before and after 2004. It discusses principles behind its transformation from 2004: the role of the central bank, sectoral governance, competition and private ownership, avoidance of a moral hazard and of policy drifts. The chapter explains factors behind banking crises. Key message: successful banks depend on successful states and clients and vice versa.

Keywords Central bank · Bank · Listing · Governance · Competition · Deposit guarantee · Related and directed lending · Populism

In 2003, Georgia's banking sector was small (Fig. 16.1) and fragmented, comprising 24 banks (down from 102 banks in 1995). Several banks were at risk of insolvency and the banking sector's earnings were stagnant. A number of banks representing a significant portion of the sector did not meet regulatory standards. Banks did not instill confidence, which translated into low deposit levels, high cash-based economy, high intermediation margins and weak credit culture. High lending costs and dearth of bankable projects perturbed lending to firms. Deficient banks-level monitoring, management, reporting and supervisory practices hindered assessment of balance sheet risks. Anti-money laundering measures were insufficient. Weak "fit and proper" regulations meant lax oversight of

D. Gvindadze, *The Transformation of Georgia from 2004 to 2012*,
https://doi.org/10.1007/978-3-031-18264-8_16

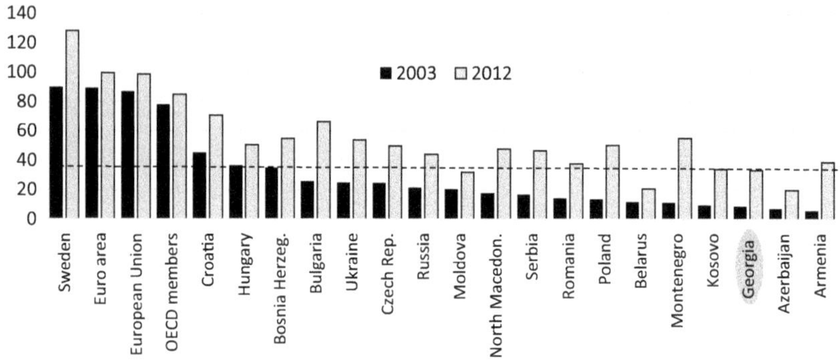

* Domestic credit to private sector by banks refers to financial resources provided to the private sector by deposit taking corporations except central banks, such as through loans, purchases of nonequity securities, and trade credits and other accounts receivable, that establish a claim for repayment.

Fig. 16.1 Domestic credit to private sector by banks (percent of GDP) in 2003 and 2012* (*Sources* Retrieved from the World Bank's database [August 2022]. International Monetary Fund, International Financial Statistics and data files, and the World Bank/OECD GDP est)

banks' owners and managers. Payment and settlement system was not developed. The absence of institutional investors and a narrow access to a market-based foreign financing restricted access to liquidity. Weak legal and procedural framework meant that courts could suspend the central bank's decisions (including decisions to withdraw banking licenses and to handle problem banks) and that banks could not properly enforce collateral. The central bank's staff was not immune from lawsuits related to the exercise of their official duties.[1]

After 2004, Georgia's banking sector was modernized and helped by an improved regulatory and operational environment. Banks enhanced their sophistication, IT savviness, service and product quality, winning international awards for best consumer, digital and mobile banking. They withstood pressures from the global financial crisis in 2008–2009 and from Russia's war against Georgia in 2008. A proper cross-sectoral asset

[1] A useful analysis of Georgia's banking system before the Revolution of Roses is offered in Georgia: Financial System Stability Assessment; IMF Country Report No. 01/210 (November 2001).

dispersion, good capital base and liquidity helped. No withdrawal restrictions were imposed and banks did not request bailouts. Georgia's banks developed relative resilience to electoral cycles and could plan long term. The vulnerabilities explained in the beginning of the chapter were reduced or eliminated. Quality of banks' shareholders improved. Georgia's state building helped significantly.

In February of 2012, the Bank of Georgia (BOG)—at the time Georgia's largest bank representing one-third of the sector—became the second foreign bank to obtain a premium listing on the London Stock Exchange (LSE). This entailed stringent financial disclosure, transparency and corporate governance standards, offered development opportunities and increased stock liquidity and the investor base expansion. BOG had first listed its shares in the form of Global Depository Receipts in November 2006—the first bank from the Caucasus and the second bank from the former Soviet Union to have done so. The premium listing in 2012 build on that pioneering deal. The turnaround of BOG started with arrival of a new Executive Chairman in 2004. It spearheaded modernization of the entire sector. This points to the importance of individuals who can be as consequential as institutions.[2]

Figure 16.2 shows evolution of Georgia's banking sector in 2004–2012.[3] Total assets of the banking sector increased from US$ 650 million to US$ 8.7 billion (CAGR 33%). Ratio of banking assets to GDP increased from 18 to 55%. Net loans increased from US$ 350 million in 2004 to US$ 4.9 billion in 2012 (CAGR 34%). Total deposits increased from US$ 370 million to US$ 4.9 billion (CAGR 33%). Shareholder equity increased from US$ 170 million in 2004 to US$ 1.44 billion in 2012 (CAGR 27%). The number of debit cards increased from less than 100,000 to more than 4 million. The number of credit cards increased from zero to 800,000. The number of ATMs increased from approximately 100 to 1900. The number of POS terminals increased from less than 500 to almost 14,000. The loan book expansion was mainly deposit-driven. Exposure to volatile funding was limited. In 2012, the non-deposit funding consisted of equity capital (42%), borrowing from international financial institutions (38%), domestic borrowing (9%),

[2] Fast forward into 2016, and Georgia's two largest banks—TBC Bank and BOG—representing two-thirds of the sector assets were listed in the LSE's premium segment.

[3] Metrics converted from GEL to US$ for ease of reference; note that in 2004–2012 GEL appreciated from approximately 2.1 GEL per US$ to 1.66 GEL per US$.

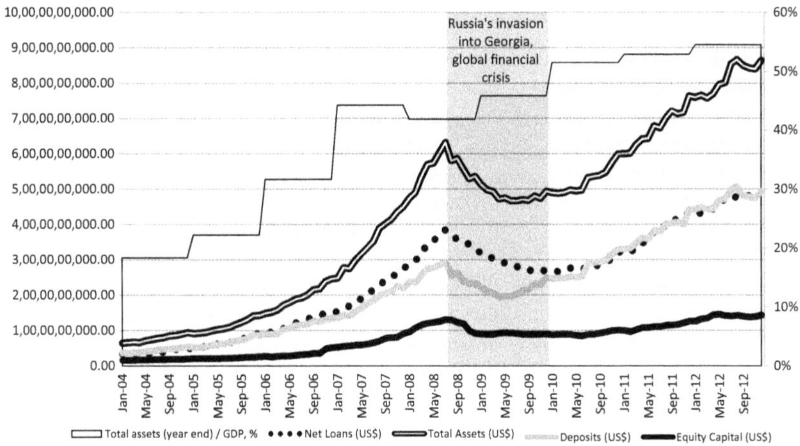

Fig. 16.2 Georgia's banking sector in 2004–2012 (*Source* National Bank of Georgia, International Monetary Fund. World Economic Outlook [2016])

borrowing from non-resident parent banks (4%) and borrowing from private external sources (7%).

Through acquisitions and organic growth, Georgia's leading banks advanced their franchise in broker-dealership, insurance, asset and wealth management, card and payment processing, investment advisory, securities and underwriting business and economic analytics. This contributed to the generally solid profitability despite conservative capital adequacy standard (approximately six times total assets to equity ratio in 2012, up from four times in 2004).[4] In 2012, Georgia's banking sector had one of the highest bank capital to assets ratios in the region (Fig. 16.3).

This transformation of Georgia's banking in 2004–2012 was helped by several factors:

- **The central bank's authority and proper governance of the sector.** The National Bank of Georgia (NBG) led on monetary, exchange rate and financial stability policies. Its leadership had no conflicts of interest and could not be held to ransom by vested interests. NBG built up credibility with commercial bankers.

[4] L. Gurgenidze (2009).

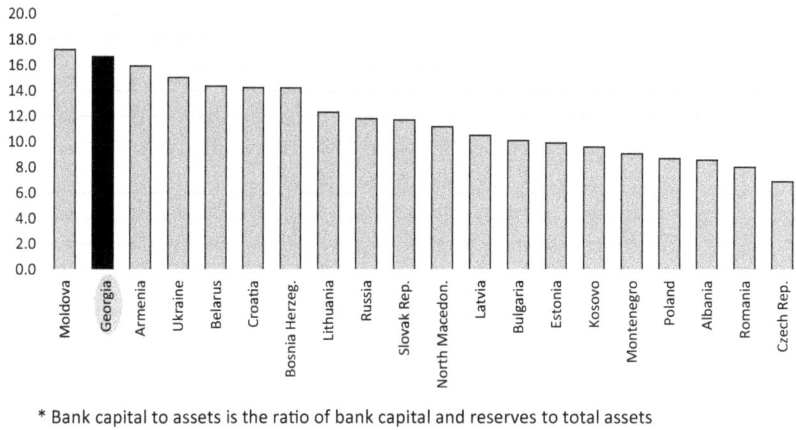

Fig. 16.3 Bank capital to assets ratio in 2012, percent* (*Sources* Retrieved from the World Bank's database [October 2020]. International Monetary Fund, financial soundness indicators)

Georgia's state building helped. In countries with weak law enforcement, central banks lack legal and institutional safeguards. Regulation alone—even good regulation—cannot prevent fraud. Law enforcement is the precondition for protection of creditor and investor rights, for successful privatizations and corporate governance transformations in the banking sector. For example, the money laundering in 2010-2014 where billions were reportedly moved from Russia involved multiple jurisdictions.[5] Can a "transit country"'s central banker unprotected by a national security apparatus challenge such schemes? Protection of decision makers against retribution is important. It must match long-term risks of the retribution.

Where the state building fails, the menu of risks in banking sectors is long:

1. Powerful businessmen own banks not to maximize shareholder value but to provide financial services to their other core

[5] The Global Laundromat: how did it work and who benefited? 20 March 2017, *The Guardian*.

non-financial businesses. This perpetuates an excessive fragmentation of banking sectors and compresses banks' profit margins. The question why would someone own a bank if such bank's return on equity (ROE) is lower than a term deposit rate becomes rhetorical as the ROE is peripheral to such bank owner's core money-making strategies.

2. A regulator cannot enforce an ultimate beneficiary owner's (UBO) transparency and quality. This undermines modern banking and sound corporate governance. Bad shareholders cheat, launder money and divert bank liquidity to related businesses. Such related businesses may be at home or abroad; they may be shell companies with no collateral if the aim is to siphon away liquidity and drive a bank into ruins. Local and international criminals may infiltrate capital of banks—in one go or through several transactions each small enough to remain below regulatory disclosure requirements—to rob and asset strip banks.
3. Depositors may wake up to an illiquid or an insolvent bank because a kleptocrat who controls the administration of justice stops servicing his debts or takes on corporate borrowers who support a rival political camp. This can toxify even a solvent bank.
4. Problem bank resolution suffers as public officials cannot decide, fearing a backlash from powerful bank owners and feeling unprotected. A bank resolution may become a backdoor for hollowing out such bank by acquiring its good assets on the cheap in the context of direct fire sales or twisted auctions.
5. Related party loans increase; they are "ever-greened" (refinanced) or come as "bullet loans" (repayment of a principal at the end of a term) to disguise asset impairments. Without a proper collateral, related party borrowers hold a leverage over regulators seeking to replace opaque shareholders. Banks where the related party lending is the norm do not compete with rivals on client solutions and product innovation because businesses they serve belong to their shareholders. Shifts from the related party to an arm's length lending entail painful business model overhauls.

Box 16.1: Banking Sector Governance—Lessons from Ukraine and Moldova

Certain Ukrainian banks established before Ukraine's Revolution of Dignity in 2014 were such banks owners' conduits for funding their related assets. Some owned banks because they did not want to rely on rivals' banks.

Transformation of Ukraine's banking sector gained pace immediately after the Revolution of Dignity despite a significant shock to Ukraine's economy due to Russia's invasion into Ukraine from 2014 (in 2014–2015, Ukraine's hryvnia depreciated against US$ by 67%; Ukraine's real GDP contracted by 16%; economic indicators (exports, industrial production, tax revenues) in Ukraine's eastern regions affected by the fighting plummeted). Led by a new, modern and courageous team in Ukraine's central bank, reforms resulted in a reduction of the number of banks from approximately 180 in 2014 to approximately 100 in 2016. The central bank was overhauled and reestablished its credibility. As part of the IMF's 2015 program and with support of Ukraine's international partners, the authorities undertook to implement measures to identify, monitor and unwind above-limit loans to insiders and to improve corporate governance in the banking sector.

Ukraine's banking depends on the modernization of state-owned enterprises and of state-owned banks. Most of all, it depends on the removal of huge risks stemming from Russia's all-out war against Ukraine.

Insufficient UBO transparency, related party lending, regulatory flaws and influence of vested interests on the administration of justice enabled massive frauds in and through Moldova's banking sector, which hit the image of the country. In 2010–2014, close to US$ 20 billion were reportedly moved through Moldova in the series of international money laundering operations collectively called "global laundromat." Abuse by banks' shareholders and regulatory flaws led to a failure, in 2014, of Moldova's three banks amounting to one-third of the sector assets. Central bank's emergency loans to these banks increased domestic public debt from 36% of GDP in 2014 to 46% of GDP in 2016 as these emergency loans were then securitized to become the liability of the ministry of finance to the central bank. The fraud resulted in a slowdown of an international budget support, in significant tightening of monetary conditions and in reduction of foreign exchange reserves. Lending opportunities shrank and large banks increased their exposures to high-yielding treasury securities.

The IMF's 2016 program in Moldova prioritized banking sector reform through strengthening of regulatory, supervisory and resolution frameworks and ending of supervisory forbearance in the face of shareholder or manager misconduct. The authorities undertook to enhance the central bank's powers and capacity to identify banks' UBOs and related party lending. Three largest banks which represented two-thirds of the sector assets and had weak corporate governance and intransparent shareholding were placed under the central bank's supervision and required to implement remedial action plans. The central bank's new modern managers, efforts by Moldova's main international partners and Moldova's improved national governance helped to improve regulatory oversight and bring new strategic and financial investors into the banking sector. Like Ukraine, Moldova is exposed to material vulnerabilities stemming from Russia's geopolitical revisionism.

Successful banks depend on successful countries and clients. Protection of reformers during and after their terms of office is key.

- **Competition.** Retention and increase of market shares by Georgian banks depended on quality of their corporate governance and on innovative products and channels. Simplified mechanics of a bank-to-bank borrower switch leveled the playing field, compressed intermediation margins and service fees. Positive international narrative on Georgia helped banks to attract quality equity investors and lenders. Foreign banks—including global brand names—not ready to commit to their Georgian operations their top talent would be unable to out-compete innovative and ambitious Georgian banks. Management boards of Georgia's largest banks listed on the London Stock Exchange have mainly Georgian composition, whereas supervisory boards include high-caliber Georgian and foreign finance, investment and management professionals.

- **Private ownership of banks.** Georgia had no state-owned and national development banks (SONDB) tasked with promotion of "strategic sectors" of the economy. This freed the budget from contingent liabilities and prevented a misallocation of resources. SONDBs generate several risks: (1) they may invite rent seeking from vested interests; governments may be unable or unwilling to confront this and may thus end up providing long-term cheap finance for projects which can be funded commercially or must not be funded at all; (2) governments may use SONDBs to enter sectors which are best served by private investors and lenders; because private investors are reluctant to compete with a quasi-public entrant, they may retrench or re-think their entry; (3) governments may use SONDBs to circumvent fiscal rules (e.g., retain a government budget deficit within certain limits while de facto increasing it through directed lending via SONDBs which is not classified as part of a government); (4) once established, SONDBs protect their mandate even when they are no longer needed and might no longer be additional to commercial banks (to paraphrase The Economist, development banks can become "solutions in search of a problem"); (5) SONDBs may engage in credit redistribution which favors political contenders representing a ruling party; this "helps" when you are in power but acts against you when you are in opposition; (6) a shareholder value maximization—the prime goal of a corporate CEO—applies more tangentially to SONDBs; (7) an overall impact and negative externalities of SONDBs are difficult to measure, not least because governments which own them are unlikely to produce reports stating that incurred costs were inefficient.[6]

  In theory, these risks can be mitigated through corporate governance and other safeguards which SONDBs in advanced countries usually possess. In developing countries, this is more difficult. Hence, (1) if SONDBs do not exist, consider avoiding them; (2) if SONDBs exist, consider corporatizing and/or privatizing them (an upfront sale to a good strategic investor might be the best option, even if such sale happens at a lower multiple to a bank's book value; an alternative—a state-led pre-privatization preparedness and corporatization plan—might take years to implement and might fall

[6] A useful perspective is provided in National Development Banks are Back in Vogue (7 March 2019) *The Economist*.

prey to changing political tides); (3) be cautious listening to experts extolling virtues of SONDBs in developing countries.

- **No deposit guarantee scheme (DGS).** Pros and cons of a DGS in Georgia were discussed, including at an open hearing in the Parliament. It was agreed that at the given stage of its development Georgia's banking sector was best served by the market discipline and the good supervision rather than by a potentially underfunded DGS. Evidence on DGSs in developing economies with evolving banking sectors is inconclusive. DGSs might create a false sense of safety, weakening scrutiny which market participants must exercise with respect to banks with which they transact. Depositors may flock to bad banks offering speculative rates because they know they will be paid back from a budget at the expense of taxpayers or from a DGS at the expense of an entire banking sector. In Georgia's rapidly evolving banking sector of 2004–2012, a DGS might have increased moral hazard and halted consolidation.
- **No policy zigzags and no populism.** Banking is a confidence-driven business vulnerable to random statements, to changes in models of economic development and in toolkits to implement them. Populists single out bankers for negative treatment that the latter often do not deserve. Georgia's authorities sought to ensure that (1) the economic model was, on balance, resilient to domestic politics and (2) bankers were not portrayed as scapegoats on matters over which they had little control.

CHAPTER 17

Territorial Development and Urbanization

Abstract This chapter explains the link between territorial development, urbanization and growth. It discusses Georgia's economic geography after the Soviet break-up. It explains principles behind Georgia's territorial development and urbanization from 2004: (1) predictability, adaptability and boldness, (2) livability of Tbilisi through harnessing its uniqueness, creating landmarks and addressing over-congestion, (3) mitigation of Tbilisi's over-dominance through development of other cities and regions, and (4) coastal development.

Keywords Territorial development · Rural exodus · Urbanization · Congestion · Urban regeneration · Coastal development

Until the 2000s, a discourse on urbanization and spatial planning often deplored a "rural exodus"—a migration of people from villages to cities. Resultant policy prescriptions aimed at rebalancing growth through stopping or reversing this exodus. This pleased protectors of a rural lifestyle, but ignored market forces, economies of scale and scope, and opportunity costs of retaining a spatial status quo. Then, the discourse started changing, with a growing acknowledgment that economic and demographic densities cannot be spread out evenly and indiscriminately and

D. Gvindadze, *The Transformation of Georgia from 2004 to 2012*,
https://doi.org/10.1007/978-3-031-18264-8_17

that instead of the over-emphasis of remote or rural communities policy-makers should (1) foster an interaction between developed and lagging areas and (2) shift from a narrow spatial targeting to a strategic approach to the territorial development and urbanization.[1] The fixation on the rural exodus started vanishing from the mainstream.

In this context, this chapter discusses four principles behind Georgia's territorial development and urbanization in 2004–2012. It showcases projects launched and/or completed in 2004–2012. A detailed review of all infrastructure projects in 2004–2012 would make this chapter much longer.

Principle 1: Predictive, Adaptive and Bold Territorial Development

Georgia inherited its territorial development from the Soviet Union. Soviet central planning, trade and industrial integration shaped Georgia's road, railway and communication networks and influenced demographic density. Georgia's geopolitical and geoeconomic realities then changed abruptly in the 1990s,

- Coastal Abkhazia region in Georgia's North-West was the best-known Soviet tourism destination attracting visitors from the Communist camp and beyond. Since the 1990s, Abkhazia is under a de facto Russian occupation. From 2004, the government accelerated development of the Ajara coast in Georgia's South-West.
- In the Soviet times, Samegrelo was a vibrant region linking the South Caucasus (Armenia, Azerbaijan, Georgia) to Russia and the European part of the Soviet Union through rail and roads. From the 1990s, Samegrelo became an impasse bordering the occupied Abkhazia. It absorbed thousands of internally displaced persons from Abkhazia. Proximity to the conflict zone led to an economic decline.
- Elevation of travel and tourism into the rank of Georgia's top priorities after 2004 depended on regional development and connectivity. Broadening of Georgia's beach and sun, winter and ski, cultural and

[1] Useful insights on the territorial and spatial planning contained in the World Development Report "Reshaping Economic Geography" (2009), World Bank.

ecotourism franchise, and development of casinos to capture potential from neighboring countries required a heavy public investment into territorial development.

- Georgia's intended transformation into a regional financial services, retail and healthcare hub with best-in-class facilities and practitioners depended on an immersive countrywide experience which depended on quality of local and international roads and airports.
- An international transport corridor vision serving to transform Georgia into the entry gate to the Caucasus and Central Asia brought in the need to enhance logistical infrastructure to benefit from addressable regional transit flows.
- End to the Soviet industrial integration hit manufacturing in Kutaisi, until recently Georgia's second largest city. Many second- and third-tier towns shrank, whereas Tbilisi's economic and demographic dominance increased as the capital city offered best opportunities. This strained Tbilisi's infrastructure and environment and resulted in the need to decongest the city to retain urban efficiency.

Georgia's predictive, adaptive and bold territorial development from 2004 created new growth pockets. It resembled a ladder with multiple rungs. Just as it is hard to climb a ladder with one or two rungs only, it is hard to sustain national growth without creating multiple growth pockets.

Principle 2: Livability of Tbilisi

Tbilisi represents a third of Georgia's population and a half of Georgia's gross domestic product. In 2012, Georgia's second largest city Batumi was 14% of Tbilisi's population (up from 11.5% in 2003). In 2004–2012, Georgia's second and third largest cities together were up to 30% of Tbilisi's population. Tbilisi's real demographic and economic dominance is traditionally stronger as not everyone living in Tbilisi for seasonal or other purposes is registered. Some residents of Georgia's small towns are farmers cultivating adjacent land plots and commercially tied to Tbilisi. Pre-COVID-19, Tbilisi attracted roughly a half of the growing number of foreign visitors to Georgia (approximately 11 million visits to Georgia in 2019, almost three times the population of Georgia).[2] In 2012, the Tbilisi International Airport accounted for 87% of all air passengers in Georgia, with the Batumi Airport accounting for the rest (by 2019, this ratio decreased to 70% largely due to the Kutaisi Airport which started operations in 2012, as discussed later in this chapter).[3]

The liveability of Tbilisi depends on harnessing its uniqueness, creating landmarks and addressing infrastructural and environmental bottlenecks.

Harness Uniqueness

Located at the heart of the Caucasus, along the historic Silk Road, Tbilisi is not an ordinary national capital. Influenced through centuries by rivalry among regional powers and empires, Tbilisi developed a unique cultural, architectural, gastronomical, artistic and behavioral identity. It formed as a melting pot for ethnicities and religions. Tbilisi is a special place for peoples of the Caucasus. Some have their ancestors born here, and others travel for business and leisure. In the Soviet years, Tbilisi was the must-visit destination for inhabitants of other Soviet republics.

From 2004, the authorities launched the "New Life of Old Tbilisi" project to comprehensively regenerate Tbilisi's historic neighborhoods. The project was scaled up toward the second half of the period explained in this book. Funded from the state budget to move fast, the project (1) provided a case study in "vertical" urban regeneration ("vertical" because the project unfolded within a defined urban perimeter and entailed a simultaneous reconstruction of all visible and underground infrastructure) and (2) crowded in private money, with local residents and others re-discovering the potential of the old neighborhoods and investing into hotels, restaurants and guest houses, multiplying the impact of the public action.

To resurrect and reimagine the past, the project was based on old maps and photos. It entailed a complex supply and logistical chain management, an engagement with local communities, a joint effort by engineers, architects, historians, private contractors, police, utility and communication companies. The approach envisaged a simultaneous replacement of an underground infrastructure (water, sewerage, drainage, communication)

[2] Geostat.

[3] Georgian Civil Aviation Agency statistics (www.gcaa.ge retrieved in August 2022).

and of outdoor lighting, structural reinforcement of buildings, rehabilitation of facades and roofing with traditional tiles, revival of wooden carved balconies and fences and beautification of public spaces. Tourists and journalists soon flocked in. Locals saw price of their real estate increased. They could sell it and buy a more spacious property or rent it out, including on Airbnb. The poverty mitigation element was real. Land market of the Old Tbilisi was galvanized. Because potential damage from illegal or incongruous construction in the (current and prospective) project perimeter increased, quality controls mattered. Political weight of the Tbilisi municipality helped.

The "New Life of Old Tbilisi" project succeeded because it was part of Georgia's state building explained in this book. The project would not succeed in a void: refurbished neighborhoods would remain idle with no tourists and because locals would not afford a meal at a restaurant; beautified facades would disguise apathy and despair of their inhabitants and the multipliers of public action would not kick in.

Create Landmarks

The Empire State Building is the international symbol of New York and the celebration of its spirit. Sydney Opera House is the symbol of Australia and one of the world's most photographed buildings. The Centre Pompidou is Paris's international landmark. Burj Khalifa is the international symbol of Dubai, the eulogy to the modern engineering. MahaNakhon skyscraper is the landmark building in Bangkok. The Interlace Apartment Building Complex in Singapore became the World Building of the Year. Landmarks have aesthetical, political and economic connotations, especially so in developing countries seeking to attract travelers, investors, journalists, TV watchers, readers and scholars.

In 2004–2012, Georgia built landmarks like a pedestrian Peace Bridge over Mtkvari River in Tbilisi with its LEDs-lit wavy glass roof, an impressive Public Service Hall with its petal-shaped roof supported by tubular stems, a glass and steel exhibition hall and a music theater in the form of two giant wine jars laying next to each other. Their symbiosis with the traditional buildings was meant to amplify Tbilisi's appeal. Landmarks defining Georgia internationally may trigger important positive externalities.

Address Over-Congestion

In 2020, the number of passenger cars per thousand inhabitants in Georgia was 316 (Tbilisi accounted for almost 40% of Georgia's passenger cars in that year).[4] In the European Union, the number of passenger cars per thousand inhabitants ranged from 379 to 779 in 2020.[5] The number of passenger cars in Tbilisi is thus likely to continue growing. Over-congestion entails environmental, emotional and health implications, lost work hours and high spending on imported fuel.

Urban de-congestion means balancing urban sprawl and densification to reduce transport and environmental bottlenecks, developing municipal transport infrastructure, enforcing engineering and aesthetic standards without delays in construction permits, preventing haphazard structures from clogging roads or destroying skylines, etc. In 2004–2012, Tbilisi progressed on these fronts, although the progress was uneven. Resources were invested in roads, bridges, overpasses and bypasses to deviate traffic from the city center. There was an interest in a light rail system in central districts not served by the metro, although high costs interfered with the plans. Partial renewal of a bus fleet did not reduce a car ridership.

Ultimately, Tbilisi's de-congestion depends on a modern public infrastructure and services in Tbilisi *and* on a bold national territorial development (principles 3 and 4 in this chapter). The former might not be a game changer without the latter.

Principle 3: Mitigation of Tbilisi's Over-Dominance

Vibrant cities are engines of growth and modernization. But can an over-dominant city become what Edward Luce in his book "The Retreat of Western Liberalism" calls a "death star" which hovers over the rest of the country, sucks in talent and capital and is parasitic on depressed and underpopulated regions?[6] What are the implications of Tbilisi's political, demographic and economic over-dominance on people in smaller towns? Do they stay put, relocate to Tbilisi or emigrate? Emigration often

[4] Geostat.

[5] Eurostat.

[6] E. Luce (2017) discusses dominance of London and Chicago and political, economic and demographic implications of such dominance.

does not mean much greener pastures or a job safety. It splits breadwinners abroad from families in Georgia. It increases vulnerability in times of distress. Think of the COVID-19 crisis in 2020 and its impact on migrants not eligible for host countries' social safety nets and unable to return home due to a disruption of travel.

The "black star" risks can be mitigated through multiplication of poles of economic growth, regeneration of cities (Batumi and Kutaisi, discussed below) or development of new economic clusters (Lazika, discussed below). This can relieve pressure on Tbilisi and foster urbanization in Georgia. This can help to discover new growth engines and increase international and domestic tourism as people explore second, third, fourth and fifth cities and their cultural, educational, urban and natural catchment areas. This can enrich the political culture by multiplying urban elites beyond Tbilisi who listen to local constituencies. Better in-country mobility through domestic tourism and other exchanges consolidates the nation. Rather than taking a high-speed East–West highway from Tbilisi to the Black Sea resort Batumi in summer, a resident of Tbilisi starts deviating from it to explore an urban, cultural and natural habitat along the route.

In 2004–2012, Georgia invested heavily into territorial development and urbanization. A comprehensive regeneration benefited towns, villages, cultural and natural heritage sites and their access infrastructure. This spending represented most of Georgia's high capital expenditure explained in Chapter 10 of this book.

Economic rates of return for infrastructure projects which transform a country's territorial development depend on multiple assumptions and are usually quantifiable ex post easier than ex ante. A sweeping change of a territorial development thus represents an act of faith, a leap into a relative unknown where the rates of return depend on individual projects' strategic fit with all other aspects of the state building.

Example of Batumi

Batumi—the capital of Ajara region in Georgia's South-West—counted around 150,000 residents after the Soviet break-up. By 2003, this number plunged to around 120,000 residents.

I visited Batumi in summer of 2003, shortly before the Revolution of Roses. Hospitality infrastructure was inexistent and investors stayed away. The centrally located Intourist hotel—the only relatively decent hotel at that time—had a glitzy worn out façade and an interior with Soviet-era furniture in rooms and long red rugs along corridors. Speeding along patchy central roads were motley Hammers and Porsches belonging to the local elite. Ajara's leader, eternally reluctant to visit Tbilisi, ruled the region as his fiefdom and addressed locals through lengthy televised monologues extalling virtues of stability. When the Revolution of Roses happened in November of 2003, he blew up a bridge linking Ajara to the rest of Georgia. When the revolution swept across Ajara in May of 2004, he fled to Russia. Had he succeeded, the blow to Georgia's statehood would be devastating.

By 2012, Batumi became one of the key investment destinations in the Caucasus, with hotels and residential construction boom, growing population and jobs. Everyone spoke of the "Batumi miracle." Batumi's population rebounded to 150,000 by 2012 and to 163,000 in 2018 by which time Batumi became Georgia's second largest city replacing Kutaisi. It prospered while most of regional towns were losing inhabitants to Tbilisi and to emigration.

Behind these trends was a major top-down public effort to develop Batumi. This included spending hundreds of millions from the budget and from international development partners' support to adapt underground infrastructure to an increased urban load capacity, to build landmarks, overhaul public spaces, reinforce and redesign the coastline, reclaim new lands along the seashore and create an international buzz. A modernized border crossing with Turkey twenty kilometers from Batumi multiplied the throughput capacity and attracted tourists and investors. It was the most futuristic border crossing in the region. The government started construction of bypass roads deviating transit traffic from centers of Batumi and other nearby seaside resorts. In 2007, Georgia's Constitutional Court moved from Tbilisi to Batumi. The government chose Batumi to host a campus of a technological university which Georgia sought to launch in cooperation with the US universities, supported through the US Millennium Challenge Program.

To promote Batumi's international brand recognition, the authorities used foreign visits and roadshows. Guided tours were arranged to explain how Batumi's turnaround was part of a broader regional development (hospitality infrastructure expansion along the Black Sea coast to the north and south of Batumi, a new nearby winter resort in Goderdzi, cultural, hospitality and transport infrastructure development in the South of Georgia to secure an alternative route from East Georgia to the Ajara seashore via Goderdzi, etc.).

Batumi acquired an independent demographic and economic momentum—the "escape velocity." The city reached an inflection point where private investment outpaced public spending. It attracted international hotel brands and offered good bed and breakfast opportunities, chic restaurants, cafés, nightclubs and casinos. Foreign nationals started to account for a large number of apartment sales. Dilapidated infrastructure, chaotic electric wires and nighttime darkness were replaced with taverns offering traditional cuisine, regenerated parks, neon lights and glittering skyscrapers. The Batumi Piazza Square became the business card of the city, featuring open-air cafés, boutique and luxury hotels and restaurants and hosting concerts by internationally celebrated singers. Tourism created thousands of jobs. Started in prime coastal locations, the urban regeneration moved inland, benefitting broader neighborhoods. Investment in botanical gardens and landmarks around Batumi made the experience immersive. In April of 2012, president of Georgia and the American real estate developer Donald Trump unveiled a plan for a Batumi Trump Tower.

Example of Kutaisi

Kutaisi is the main town of Georgia's most populous region of Imereti and the ancient capital of the Kingdom of Georgia, with monuments inscribed on the UNESCO World Heritage List, cultural and natural landmarks. Kutaisi's location makes it a nodal point of a domestic and cross-border transport network. Kutaisi is at the center of any "hub and spoke" structure of economic integration in Western Georgia. It is 90 kilometers away from the Black Sea, located on Georgia's East–West highway which leads to Abkhazia some 100 kilometers to the North-West. A successful Imereti might facilitate a westward shift of Georgia's center of gravitation and enhance the national self-awareness by better exposing citizens—including officials in Tbilisi—to diverse geo-cultural experiences.

After the Soviet break-up, Kutaisi was Georgia's second largest city with quarter million inhabitants. Its population reduced to 180,000 in 2003. Soviet-era industrial infrastructure (light and heavy machine building, chemicals, food processing, tractor, truck and motor engineering, building materials, etc.) laid idle. Unemployment increased.

Many left for Tbilisi and abroad. Municipal infrastructure decayed and tourists bypassed Kutaisi. No holistic understanding of Imereti's potential existed before 2004. Marketing effort was almost zero.

From 2004 to 2005, improvement of Kutaisi's infrastructure accelerated, including urban renewal in the downtown. To divert the increasingly heavy East–West highway traffic from Kutaisi, the authorities negotiated international funding for the Kutaisi bypass. Re-discovery and rehabilitation of cultural heritage sites in and around Kutaisi and promotion of Imereti's natural heritage unfolded in parallel. Improved secondary and local roads enhanced Kutaisi's links within the region.

In 2011, the parliament was partially relocated from Tbilisi to Kutaisi. MPs started holding sessions in both cities. Cabinet of ministers started working partially from its new seat in Kutaisi. Investors started discovering Imereti's investment opportunities. In May of 2012, Kutaisi hosted its first military parade to celebrate Georgia's Independence Day.

A new Kutaisi International Airport started providing cheap international connections. Price differential between Tbilisi and Kutaisi airports was sufficient for budget travelers from Tbilisi to travel to Kutaisi to take low-cost flights to Europe. The Kutaisi Airport became the first international airport with cost-efficient airline services in the South Caucasus. It unlocked mobility opportunities for students, seasonal workers and other low budget travelers. Low airport charges and incentives, open sky policy with the European Union and no night flight restriction spurred growth in the number of passengers. The Kutaisi Airport started in 2012 by serving 13,000 passengers for 68 flights. It served 406,000 passengers for 1822 flights in 2017.[7] Seeing *Kutaisi* at arrivals and departures boards at airports of Barcelona and Milano stirred disbelief in the early days.

In parallel, the authorities started rehabilitation of Tskhaltubo, a spa resort next to Kutaisi. Known for its balneotherapy, treatment of respiratory, skin, circulatory and metabolic diseases, and featuring many bathhouses, hotels and sanatoriums, scenic caves and natural reserves, Stalinist-era, Roman and Gothic architecture, Tskhaltubo had been a famous destination in the Soviet times. Then, in the 1990s, thousands of internally displaced persons from Abkhazia were relocated to Tskhaltubo's sanatoriums. The resort disappeared from tourists' radars. From 2010 to 2011, the authorities spent budget funds and secured the

[7] Kutaisi Airport web site, www.kutaisi.aero.

World Bank's support to regenerate Tskhaltubo and its surroundings. A search for private investors into the hospitality infrastructure unfolded parallel to plans to beautify facades and public spaces, improve roads and street lighting, replace underground infrastructure and regenerate parks. Tskhaltubo's brand name recognition was expected to help.

The relocation of the parliament to Kutaisi was reversed after 2012. Unlike Batumi, Kutaisi did not reach the "escape velocity." Its population declined to 140,000 inhabitants in 2019. At 40%, the demographic decline of the Kutaisi municipality in 1994–2019 was twice the national average.[8]

Principle 4: Coastal Development, Lazika

Developed coasts integrated into the regional and global economy drive cosmopolitanism and openness. Economic and demographic growth of coastlines usually outpaces growth elsewhere. International trade in goods is mainly carried by sea. Most of the world's largest cities are coastal cities or located close to important water routes and logistical infrastructure (Table 17.1).

Examples of the United States, China and Turkey illustrate urban, demographic and economic significance of coasts.

- In the **United States**, of top-thirty urban centers by population, 19 are coastal or have a maritime access. Of top-ten urban centers, two are landlocked and others are coastal, with concentration on the East and West coasts.[9] In 2018, states along the East and West coasts represented approximately 55% of the national GDP. If we add to the two coasts GDP generated in coastal states of the Gulf of Mexico, we arrive at two-thirds of the national GDP of the United States generated in coastal states. This percentage increases further if we add states within the Great Lakes Basin.[10] More than a half of the United States' population lives near coasts.

[8] Geostat, Population as of 1 January by regions and self-governed units, thousands.

[9] European Commission, Global Human Settlement Database, Country Fact Sheets https://ghsl.jrc.ec.europa.eu/; own analysis.

[10] Bureau of Economic Analysis, US Department of Commerce, own calculations.

Table 17.1 Proximity of the largest cities to oceans, seas and rivers

*World's largest cities**	*Proximity to ocean/sea/river***
Tokyo, Japan	Coastal city, Tokyo Bay
Delhi, India	Landlocked
Shanghai, China	Coastal city, East China Sea
São Paolo, Brazil	Coastal city, South Atlantic Ocean
Mexico City, Mexico	Landlocked; located in the lower narrower part of Mexico, almost equdistant from the Gulf of Mexico and the Pacific Ocean
Dhaka, Bangladesh	Landlocked
Cairo, Egypt	Near the Nile Delta, River Nile, close to the Mediterranean Sea, ports and the Suez
Mumbai, India	Coastal city, Artabian Sea
Beijing, China	Landlocked, close to the Yellow Sea
New York, USA	Coastal City, Atlantic Ocean
Osaka, Japan	Coastal City, Osaka Bay
Chongqing, China	Landlocked
Shenzhen, China	Coastal city, South China Sea
Karachi, Pakistan	Coastal city, Arabian Sea
Istanbul, Turkey	The Bosphorus Strait; Black Sea, Sea of Marmara, Aegean Sea, Mediterranean Sea
Buenos Aires, Argentina	Coastal city, South Atlantic Ocean
Kolkata, India	Hooghly River, within the lower Ganges Delta, close to the Bay of Bengal; Port of Kolkata is India's oldest port and its only major riverine port
Lagos, Nigeria	Coastal city, Gulf of Guinea
Kinshasa, DRC	Landlocked
Manila, Philipinnes	Coastal city, Manila Bay
Rio de Janeiro, Brasil	Coastal city, South Atlantic Ocean
Tianjin, China	Coastal city, Yellow Sea
Guangzhou, Guangdong, China	Coastal city, South China Sea
Los Angeles, USA	Coastal city, Pacific Ocean
Moscow, Russia	Landlocked
Lahore, Pakistan	Landlocked
Bangalore, India	Landlocked
Paris, France	Landlocked
Bogota, Columbia	Landlocked
Jakarta, Indonesia	Coastal city, Jakarta Bay
Chennai (Madras), India	Coastal city, Bay of Bengal
Lima, Peru	Coastal city, Pacific Ocean
Bangkok, Thailand	Coastal city, Gulf of Thailand

(continued)

Table 17.1 (continued)

*World's largest cities**	*Proximity to ocean/sea/river***
Seoul, Republic of Korea	Han River, city center approximately 60 kilometers from the Yellow Sea
Hyderabad, India	Landlocked
Tehran, Iran	Landlocked, close to the Caspian Sea
London, UK	Thames River, English Channel, North Sea, Atlantic Ocean
Ho Chi Minh City, Vietnam	Coastal city, South China Sea
Chengdu, China	Landlocked
Nanjing, Jiangsu, China	Close to Shanghai, East China Sea
Luanda, Angola	Coastal city, South Atlantic Ocean
Ahmadabad, India	Approx. 80 kilometers from the Gulf of Khambhat on the Arabian Sea coast of India
Dar es Salaam, Tanzania	Coastal city, Indian Ocean

*For the list of cities, consulted: The World's Cities in 2018—Data Booklet (ST/ESA/SER.A/417) UN Department of Economic and Social Affairs, Population Division (2018)
**Proximity to ocean / sea / river - own analysis, for depictive purposes only

- Of top-thirty most populous urban centers in **China**, 18 are coastal or close to the coastline, forming industrial, trade and economic clusters with coastal areas. The contrast is starker in case of top-ten most populous urban centers, of which eight have important maritime access. China's coastal provinces drive growth and employment. These provinces—mainly the Bohai Basin, the Pearl River Delta and the Yangtze River Delta—represent less than a fifth of China's area but generated more than a half of the national GDP in 2005. China's opening to foreign trade and investment boosted coastal areas that became gateways to overseas markets, hosting international market-oriented industries. At the same time, many landlocked areas stumbled.[11]
- Of top-thirty most populous urban centers in **Turkey**, 17 are located at or close to the coast. Of Turkey's top-ten most populous urban centers, six are coastal and four landlocked. Turkey's largest city Istanbul is the transcontinental city on the Bosporus Strait connecting the Black Sea to the Sea of Marmara, Aegean Sea

[11] World Development Report (2009) "Reshaping Economic Geography," *The World Bank*.

and the Mediterranean Sea. Istanbul alone amounts to more than a half of the total population of Turkey's ten most populous urban centers and represents almost one-third of Turkey's GDP.

How does Georgia fare in comparison with these trends? Georgia's Black Sea coastline is approximately 315 kilometers long, of which approximately 190 kilometers are in the occupied Abkhazia and the rest in Georgia's other three regions with access to the Black Sea—Samegrelo-Zemo Svaneti, Guria and Ajara. There is no accurate account of Abkhazia's current demographic or economic trends, though in the last three decades the region declined grotesquely on both fronts. Population of eight coastal municipalities along Georgia's Black Sea coast (outside of Abkhazia) was approximately 15% of Georgia's population in 2019. Even if we add to this the population of adjacent municipalities with no direct coastline access, the ratio increases marginally to 20%. The Batumi municipality contributes significantly to the coastal demographics and economy. Without Batumi, population of the other seven coastal municipalities would represent approximately 10% of Georgia's population.

In the last three decades, density (population per one square kilometer) in Samegrelo-Zemo Svaneti and Guria reduced by more than the countrywide decrease in density of population. Density decrease in Ajara was slightly lower than for the entire Georgia due to the development of Batumi and of its surroundings. In the Soviet times, rail and roads connecting the South Caucasus with the European part of the Soviet Union passed through Samegrelo. Samegrelo was vibrant and outward looking. With the occupation of Abkhazia, Samegrelo suffered significantly. Despite direct access to the Black Sea, Samegrelo's population mainly lives inland and the coastline is largely unused.

A combined GDP of Ajara, Samegrelo-Zemo Svaneti and Guria represented only 16% of Georgia's GDP in 2018. Combined GDP of Samegrelo-Zemo Svaneti and of Guria represented only 8% of the GDP, stretching along more than a half of Georgia's Black Sea coast (excluding the occupied Abkhazia section of the coast).[12]

And yet, Georgia's Black Sea coast is (1) the only maritime entry gate and a recreational hub for 17 million inhabitants of the South Caucasus and for international visitors in Georgia; (2) the stepping-stone

[12] Geostat, April 2020.

for 70 million plus inhabitants of Northern Iran (excluding Teheran) and Central Asia; (3) the transit point for trade flows between the Caucasus and Europe/rest of the world, between Central Asia and Europe/rest of the world and between landlocked Western China and Europe (Georgia is the only country in the region which has free trade agreements with both China and the European Union; it is part of the Silk Road and can benefit from China's "One Belt One Road" initiative).

In 2011, Georgia announced construction of the city of Lazika on the Black Sea coast, next to the occupation line separating Abkhazia from the rest of Georgia (Lazika was an ancient kingdom in Georgia's West which extended into Abkhazia). The city of Lazika migrated to the list of top priority projects. Within a decade, the authorities imagined Lazika as a financial, commercial and trade center. Lazika would provide an urban barrier to Russia's further invasion into Georgia.

Located 30 kilometers from Zugdidi, Lazika was to boost development of the Samegrelo region of which Zugdidi is the center. It was to foster economic re-integration with Abkhazia. To provide investors with legal and operational safeguards, including English law model for commercial transactions, Lazika was imagined as a "Charter City" governed by its own rules.

The authorities invested in infrastructure and started sounding out private investors. Lazika's public service hall, access roads, a futuristic sea pier, a sea boulevard with palm trees, a long pedestrian bridge with scenic view of a river delta and modern public spaces sprang up from nowhere. Aqua Lazika—at that time one of the most advanced water parks in Eastern Europe—opened in summer of 2012. Investors built waterfront hotels. The buzz grew louder by the day. Local land and real estate markets were galvanized. Lazika started to host youth camps and seaside festivals, some sponsored by the authorities. The place started becoming hip—next to the occupation line and a year after its launch in 2011.

To enhance Georgia's geostrategic stake and to benefit from larger addressable transit flows, the authorities announced construction of the Lazika deep-sea port (local geology allows a 20 meter depth close to the shore). The port was to add to capacity of Georgia's existing ports, none of which was deep-sea. Panamax and capesize vessel traffic through Lazika (which Georgia's other ports at that time could not handle) was to change the port economics and reduce marine shipment costs. It was to foster large dry bulk and container flows additional to the existing ports capacity, with possible extension by a liquid terminal. The main railway line was to be extended to the port. Lazika was to have a free economic zone. Based on international experience (e.g., the world's largest intermodal hub in Dubai, including a free trade zone, and the Tanger Med—the largest deep-sea port in Africa integrated with a free trade zone), the government saw Lazika as part of a broader vision for the regional transport and freight logistics.

Lazika depended on transshipment volumes which, in turn, depended on Georgia's state-building and strategic corridor promotion. The causality was dual. Because of its geopolitical angle, the project depended on the backing from the government and from international allies.

Lazika was to be part of the regional effort involving construction of an airport in the coastal town of Poti some 30 kilometers south of Lazika (the airport was to provide an all-weather 24/7 service to Samegrelo-Zemo Svaneti and nearby municipalities) and regeneration of the coast from Lazika to Kulevi, midway from Poti. Meanwhile, a rehabilitated 130-kilometer road shrank travel time from Zugdidi to Mestia from more than six to three hours. The government invested in a high-altitude town Mestia and other areas of Upper Svaneti (the UNESCO World Heritage Site) to improve municipal and ski infrastructure and attract private investors. Upper Svaneti soon attracted thousands of visitors, including through the Mestia Airport opened in 2010. Lazika, Upper Svaneti, Kutaisi, Batumi, Goderdzi, Poti, etc.—these and other projects implemented or started in 2004–2012 were expected to amplify each other.

After 2013, the Lazika project slowed down and then stopped.

CHAPTER 18

Dollarization: A Thought Framework

Abstract This chapter explains whether and under which conditions Georgia can benefit from a unilateral adoption of EUR or US$ as its sole legal tender. This leads to a discussion of common currency areas, of trade-offs between exchange rate arrangements, financial openness and monetary independence, of transaction costs of international trade, of trade-offs between a nominal and internal devaluation, of mechanics of conversion from a national to an international currency and of its impact on competitiveness and on borrowing costs.

Keywords Dollarization · Euroization · Optimum currency area · Impossible trinity · Eurozone

Georgia's real and financial sector balance sheets are de facto partially dollarized. Most of long-term savings are in US$ or EUR. Large contracts—purchase of apartments, cars, furniture, etc.—are often indexed to US$. In 2012, deposit dollarization in Georgia stood at 64% (86% in 2003) and loan dollarization at 68% (87% in 2003). Public debt

Whereas this book explains the period until 2012, this chapter—given its theoretical and forward-looking nature—uses data till 2020.

D. Gvindadze, *The Transformation of Georgia from 2004 to 2012*, https://doi.org/10.1007/978-3-031-18264-8_18

stock was mainly in hard currency due to borrowings from international development partners and Eurobond issuances.

Can a unilateral replacement of the Georgian Lari (GEL) with US$ or EUR—a shift from the de facto to a de jure dollarization or euroization—promote stability and growth? Can it support demand-side economic policies, eliminate inflation bias of the monetary policy, contribute to the financial sector and capital market development?

In 2004–2012, this topic rose interest without moving into the mainstream. I explain pitfalls, benefits and preconditions for a dollarization and euroization in Georgia. What follows is a thought framework and not an academic research. For simplicity, I use *dollarization* and *euroization* interchangeably.

Of 27 European Union (EU) countries, 19 are in the Eurozone. Non-EU countries in Europe which use EUR are Kosovo, Andorra, Vatican, Montenegro, Monaco and San Marino. No European country has adopted US$. Imagine Georgia unilaterally replacing GEL for EUR, effectively joining the EU common currency area without the EU or the Eurozone membership. Economic literature points to four conditions under which countries might benefit from joining a monetary union: extensive intra-union trade, labor mobility, symmetricity of shocks and a fiscal redistribution mechanism.[1] I review these conditions in the context of the Eurozone and add a Georgian angle:

1. **Extensive intra-union trade**. The Eurozone countries trade more with each other than with the rest of the world (Fig. 18.1). In 2002, when EUR began to circulate, intra-Eurozone exports were higher than extra-Eurozone exports for almost all member states. The intra-regional trade integration thus *preceded* adoption of the EUR. In contrast, in 2004–2012, Georgia's export to the EU was approximately 20% of its total exports and import to the EU was approximately 30% of its total imports.[2]
2. **Labor mobility**. Georgia's migration statistics is not fully comparable with the Eurostat's intra-EU labor mobility data. Georgia's blue collar and seasonal workers or personal care aides in the EU and

[1] Discussion of *optimum currency areas* in Caves, Frankel, Jones (2002).

[2] Geostat.

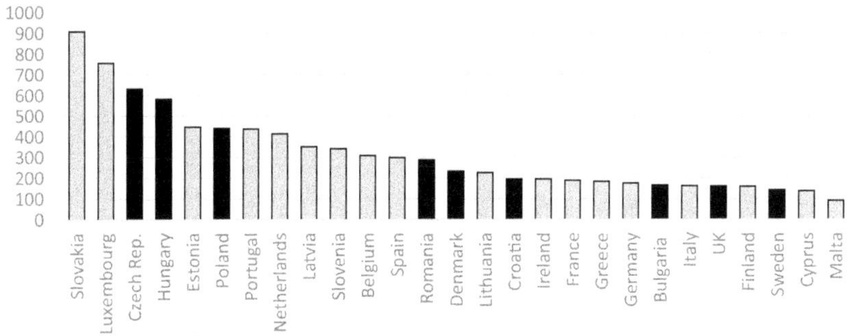

Note: Black bars represent the EU members which are not part of the Eurozone
Source: Eurostat, Comext table DS-063319 ("EUROSTAT statistics explained - Intra-EU trade in goods - recent trends), http://ec.europa.eu/eurostat/statistics-explained/index.php/Intra-EU_trade_in_goods_-_recent_trends#Intra-EU_trade_in_goods_by_Member_State (August 2018)

Fig. 18.1 Intra-EU exports divided by extra-EU exports of goods, × 100 (the EU, 2002)

elsewhere do not disclose their means of income generation; departures of entire households affect statistical trails; illegal migrants are below radars of statisticians. Still, the role of Georgia's migrants is significant (Fig. 18.2). In 2004–2012, Georgia's workers' remittances in US$ increased 12-fold despite the global financial crisis in 2008–2009 and the Eurozone's economic crisis. From 2017, the EU abolished visa obligations for Georgia's citizens traveling to the Schengen zone for a short stay (without the right to work)—an important political step which fosters mobility. But this pales compared to the freedom of movement of citizens—one of the EU's four fundamental freedoms (others being freedom for movement of goods, services and capital). Note that the geographic mobility of labor is lower in the EU than in the United States where it plays a stronger role reducing economic differences across states.[3]

3. **Symmetricity of shocks**. The Eurozone's institutional, monetary and redistribution policies aim to synchronize business cycles and

[3] Z. Gáková and L. Dijkstra. European Union Regional Policy no. 02/2008, Labour mobility between the regions of the EU-27 and a comparison with the USA. https://ec.europa.eu/regional_policy/sources/docgener/focus/2008_02_labour.pdf (retrieved in February 2021).

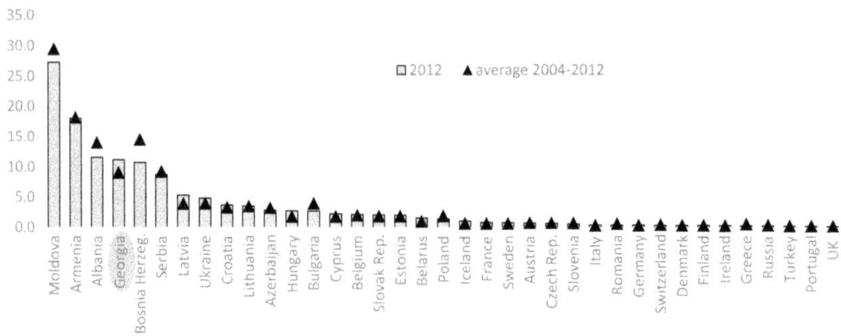

Fig. 18.2 Personal remittances received, percent of GDP, ranked by 2012 ratios (*Source* The World Bank. World Development Indicators [August 2018]. World Bank staff estimates based on IMF balance of payments data, and World Bank and OECD GDP estimates)

promote convergence among its member states. Still, the European sovereign debt crisis since the end of 2009 impacted asymmetrically the EU countries with diverse income levels and economic structures. This temporarily reignited a debate on whether the Eurozone was an optimum currency area. The EU and the European Central Bank (ECB) then supported the EU member states and strengthened institutional safeguards against sovereign and banking crises. In 2012, the ECB president promised to do "whatever it takes" to save the Euro. The EU adopted mutual support measures. A unilateral euroization in the absence of the Eurozone membership and of an access to the EU's mutual support mechanisms might constrain policy flexibility without delivering a sufficient risk mitigation in times of crises. Georgia's low-income per capita and low economic complexity might entail a asymmetric impact of shocks (Fig. 18.3).

4. **Fiscal redistribution**. Despite its many wealth redistribution mechanisms, on the measure of fiscal federalism Eurozone is behind the United States. Calls for the EU to scale up its fiscal arsenal increased as the region fought the COVID-19 crisis from 2020. France and Germany proposed the European coronavirus recovery fund raising billions in common EU debt to distribute it to member states in the form of grants. This is not a fiscal union with a centralized fiscal governance, but the thinking on enhancing the EU's redistribution

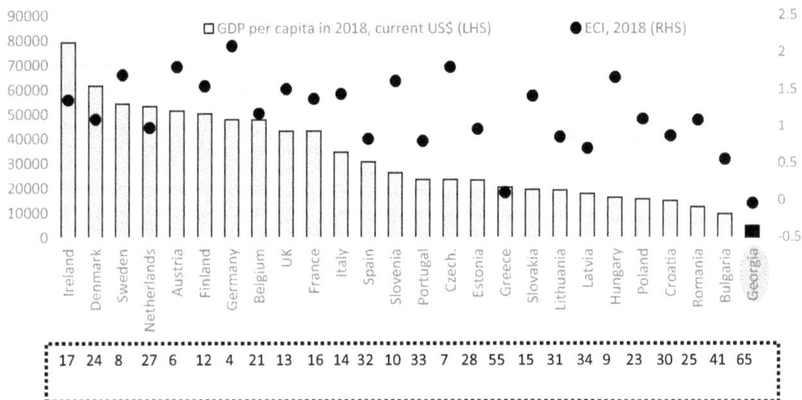

The Economic Complexity Index (ECI) ranks countries based on diversity and complexity of their exports. ECI provides a useful measure of economic development. Source: The Growth Lab at Harvard University. The Atlas of Economic Complexity. http://www.atlas.cid.harvard.edu

Fig. 18.3 GDP per capita and economic complexity in 2018 (the EU, Georgia)

policies has a strong momentum.[4] Georgia's unilateral euroization would not provide access to the EU's fiscal redistribution. But, linked to the EU through the Association Agreement, Georgia benefits from the EU's and international development partners' grants and loans whose volumes can be material in times of crises.

Further considerations in the context of the unilateral dollarization or euroization:

According to the **"Impossible Trinity" principle**, a country cannot have simultaneously fixed exchange rates, financial openness and monetary independence. Of these three attributes, it can chose two only.[5] A floating exchange rate thus allows a financial openness and a monetary independence. Imagine Georgia replacing GEL with EUR or US$, effectively fixing its exchange rate. Faced with a regional economic crisis, will it sacrifice monetary independence, fixed exchange rate or financial openness? *A sacrifice of the monetary independence* means a shift

[4] Is the Franco-German plan Europe's "Hamiltonian" moment? EU coronavirus recovery fund proposal puts fiscal union back on the agenda (*Financial Times*, 21 May 2020).

[5] Caves, Frankel, Jones (2002).

of an entire responsibility to fiscal authorities. Abrupt fiscal adjustments require political capital and wisdom, ability to modify public spending quickly and a public borrowing headroom. All this in the absence of the domestic monetary policy's contribution to economic stabilization within and across business cycles which might not be aligned with business cycles of countries setting policies for EUR or US$. With no central bank acting as lender of last resort, the dollarization or euroization may impact liquidity provision to the banking system. Fiscal authorities would be expected to issue a EUR or US$ denominated debt or raise taxes. Reliance on international financial institutions would increase, at least initially. *A sacrifice of the fixed exchange rate*—reintroduction of GEL—may disrupt sovereign and private sector balance sheets. With liabilities in the hard currency and assets in the reintroduced GEL, brace for bankruptcies and insolvencies. *A sacrifice of the financial openness*—introduction of capital controls—will affect investment and growth. It will hit Georgia's investment-led convergence with the EU and Georgia's regional economic hub vision.

Transaction costs of international trade and degree of monetary independence. By 2017, Georgia's merchandise trade turnover (sum of merchandise exports and imports) represented 71% of GDP, up from 34% in 2000. Georgia's trade openness in 2017 was the same as in the Eurozone (70%) and in the EU (68%) and higher than in neighbors and important trade partners: Turkey (46% in 2017), Russia (37% in 2017), Azerbaijan (59% in 2017) and Armenia (56% in 2017).[6] Regional crises and economic policies in the EU and the US influence the GEL exchange rate. Regional currencies fluctuate against EUR and US$ (Fig. 18.4). Georgia is a small open economy, so its monetary and exchange rate policies are on the receiving end of such external developments. In other words, Georgia's monetary independence is not full even in the conditions of the floating exchange rate. Can the unilateral dollarization or euroization reduce transaction costs of international trade without imposing an excessive straightjacket on policymakers?

Nominal vs. internal devaluation. A floating currency cushions external shocks. Imagine a depreciation of the Turkish lira. A floating GEL may depreciate. This will affect public and private sector balance

[6] Trade openness is the sum of merchandise exports and imports of a country divided by the value of its GDP, all in current US$. *Source* World trade Organisation and World Bank GDP estimates.

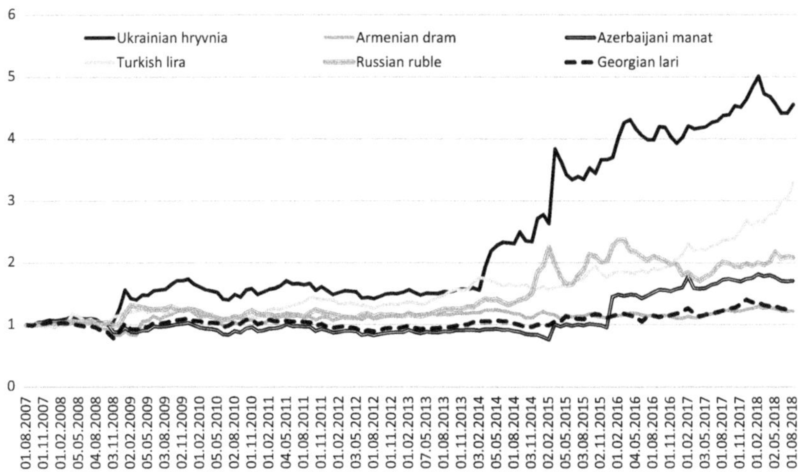

Fig. 18.4 Fluctuation of regional currencies against EUR in 2007–2018 (normalized, August 2007 exchange rate = 1) (*Source* Central banks)

sheets and might result in deleveraging and in a real output loss. The nominal GEL depreciation might increase domestic inflation and thus trigger appreciation of a real exchange rate, offsetting a temporary competitiveness boost from a weaker nominal exchange rate. Now imagine that GEL is fixed to EUR, so Georgia's competitiveness *vis-à-vis* Turkey cannot be restored through a nominal exchange rate depreciation. External competitiveness must then be restored through an *internal devaluation*—a real exchange rate depreciation through lower nominal domestic salaries and prices. In a low growth low demand context, forced reduction of prices and salaries—the untested measure in Georgia—might trigger deflation. Deflation affects growth through an expectation channel (if prices are to fall, households and firms delay spending and investment) and increases a *real* value of debt in the economy. This triggers the same adverse balance sheet impact as in the case of the nominal GEL depreciation, albeit with a time lag. The reduction of nominal salaries amplifies a political and administrative strain. Households might be more tolerant of the nominal exchange rate adjustment than of the reduction of their nominal incomes.

Mechanics and impact of conversion to EUR and access to liquidity in times of crises. Georgia's productivity is lower than in the Eurozone. Georgia's 2020 GDP per capita was approximately US$ 4,400 whereas simple average of the Eurozone countries' 2020 GDPs per capita was approximately US$ 40,000 (ranging from US$ 18,000 to US$ 115,000). Pre-adoption of EUR, do we peg GEL to EUR at an existing exchange rate, or do we set another (weaker) conversion rate reflective of the mentioned productivity differential? Would a failure to do the latter result in a permanent competitiveness loss? Will such conversion rate be accepted politically and how would it affect public and private sectors' balance sheets? To introduce EUR or US$ as sole legal tender, a country needs to be generating, on net basis, hard currency. Georgia has been running structural current account deficits funded by foreign investment and borrowing. Any unexpected stop of these capital inflows would result in an external funding gap. If the exchange rate is fixed, international reserves must be sufficient to weather the impact.

Unilateral adoption of EUR and market borrowing costs. Figure 18.5 depicts long-term government bond yields for certain EU countries. In February of 2012, yields of Greek bonds reached 30% (in the same period, yield to maturity on Georgia's 10-year Eurobond was less than 7%). German bond yields compressed to 1.85% from more than 3% a year ago because German policies were perceived as more credible and German economic structure and export-orientation benefitted from the monetary union. The divergence in bond yields happened *despite* the Eurozone countries sharing EUR and *because* some questioned the Eurozone as the optimum currency area. Bottom line: adoption of EUR alone does not entail an automatic convergence in borrowing costs. Note that (1) the Eurozone countries' borrowing costs might converge if and when they mutualize debt issuances and (2) borrowing in own currency—EUR in this case—has advantages over borrowing in "other people's money" as this might reduce exchange rate and credit risks.

This chapter's overview of advantages and disadvantages of dollarization or euroization points to many unknowns and trade-offs. Two circumstances might reignite the debate on the adoption of EUR or US$ by Georgia: (1) the EU membership and (2) a significant irrevocable strengthening of the regional hub orientation.

The EU membership would reduce many of Georgia's vulnerabilities, triggering infinitely better outcomes than suggested by economics alone. A well-managed EU member state benefitting from the EU's redistribution policies can fast-track an investment-led convergence with its wealthier neighbors. Note the experience of Estonia, Latvia and Lithuania

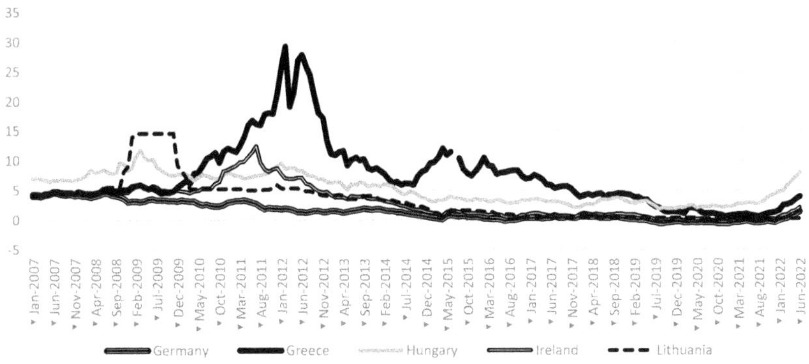

Fig. 18.5 Long-term interest rates in the EU countries—2007–2022 (Long-term interest rates refer to government bonds maturing in ten years) (*Source* OECD [2022], "Long-term interest rates" (indicator), https://doi.org/10.1787/662d712c-en [accessed on 11 August 2022])

during the financial crisis of 2008–2009. Supporting currency pegs with EUR until adoption of EUR was key to the three Baltic states' anti-crisis strategies (Estonia adopted EUR in 2011, Latvia in 2014 and Lithuania in 2015). Debates on whether to maintain the currency pegs or to foster rebalancing through currency devaluation were both political and economic. Adjustments materialized through internal devaluations, including fiscal adjustments and nominal wage adjustments in public and private sectors. External support, including from the EU, played an important role. Peak-to-through real output contractions in 2007–2010 were significant: close to 20% in Estonia and Latvia and close to 15% in Lithuania (in Georgia, peak-trough real output contraction was 3.6%).[7]

A significant irrevocable strengthening of Georgia's regional transhipment, logistical, service and economic hub orientation. An international investor interest is Georgia's national security asset. If the unilateral adoption of EUR or US$ can significantly foster the regional hub orientation, the debate thereon makes sense. Preconditions for Georgia's such regional function are (1) a permanently conducive regional geopolitics and domestic politics and (2) a resilient competitive edge in areas of national governance, regulation, economic decision-making,

[7] International Monetary Fund's World Economic Outlook database (April 2018).

administration of justice, quality of public institutions and services and protection of property rights. But bear in mind that even Singapore—a global financial and transhipment hub straddling intense commercial shipping routes and the symbol of what Georgia of 2004–2012 sought to achieve—has own currency (Singapore Dollar) and operates an exchange rate-based monetary policy in which the monetary authority manages the nominal effective exchange rate of the Singapore Dollar against a basket of currencies.

CHAPTER 19

Parliamentary Elections in 2012

Abstract This chapter explains reasons behind the United National Movement's defeat in the 2012 parliamentary elections: Georgia's relations with Russia, a difficulty of staying in power beyond two consecutive terms, the personality of the leader of the opposition, Georgia's social contract of 2004–2012, a prison abuse scandal and the tragedy of a drowned toddler, the Georgian Dream's economic, geopolitical and democratic promise.

Keywords Elections · Social contract · Prison scandal · Political legacy · Electoral promise

In the parliamentary elections on 1 October 2012, the United National Movement (UNM) in power since the Revolution of Roses of 2003 was defeated by the Georgian Dream (GD) coalition formed around Mr. Bidzina Ivanishvili, Georgia's richest man. Before entering Georgia's politics a year before the elections and uniting around him many fractious anti-UNM groups, Mr. Ivanishvili had been running the largest charity in Georgia. This, together with Mr. Ivanishvili's reclusive lifestyle in his native village, had earned him the image of a grand mythical benefactor. At that time, Mr. Ivanishvili's net worth according to Forbes was US$ 6.4

D. Gvindadze, *The Transformation of Georgia from 2004 to 2012*,
https://doi.org/10.1007/978-3-031-18264-8_19

billion—40% of Georgia's 2012 GDP. He had accumulated wealth mainly in Russia.

Of 150 parliamentary seats, 85 went to the GD and 65 to the UNM. This started a painful political transition where a clash of characters was amplified by opposite views on almost all issues. Amid international statements on the elections being the step toward the consolidation of Georgia's democracy, dramas unfolded at personal and institutional levels.

The elections of 1 October 2012 led to the first orderly transfer of power in Georgia's post-Soviet history. Politicians reveal the true extent of their addiction to power not after landslide electoral victories, but when facing risks of electoral losses, especially when such losses threaten personal safety. Upholding electoral democracy in 2012, the UNM passed an important test.

Reasons behind the UNM's electoral defeat are complex:

1. **Russia's military invasion into Georgia in 2008 and Russia's hostility towards Georgia before and after that invasion** scarred Georgia, destabilized and polarized its politics and its society. After the 2008 war, certain voices—cautious and politically correct appeasers, procrastinators and mercantilists, omniscient experts and Russia's influence agents—tried to split the blame between Russia and Georgia (Russia-laid-the-trap-but-Georgia-fell-into-it type of a nonsense). This was empirically dishonest and strategically myopic. The failure of the international community to set the record straight in 2008 and to start ringing loud alarm bells weakened the authorities in Tbilisi, empowered Russia's war against Ukraine from 2014 and Russia's all-out war against the West in Ukraine from 2022. It took the big tragedy in Europe for the discourse on the 2008 war to explicitly acknowledge that Georgia was the first victim of Russia's geopolitical revisionism.
2. **It is difficult to be in power beyond two consecutive electoral terms** unless (1) performance is spotless and (2) an electoral governance is strongly tweaked in incumbent's favor. On (1), Georgia's transformation in 2004–2012 was not mistake-free, as explained below. On (2), the 2012 electoral level playing field was not perfect, but it existed because the UNM's incumbency advantage was offset by the GD leader's status and wealth in the context of immature public institutions and of a weak enforcement of campaign finance laws.

3. **The UNM's social contract**—meritocracy, no tolerance to crime and corruption in exchange for fast growth and modernization—entailed a radical social and behavioral transformation which lowered the "threshold of intolerance" for the government's action. The government's "Teflon coating" came off soon after 2004. A push-back from certain segments of the society (criminal underworld, entrenched elites, civil servants laid off in the context of the public sector reform or of the fight against corruption, certain businesses which lost privileged treatment, citizens outstripped by the pace of the transformation, etc.) was visceral and cerebral. Georgia's transformation upset those who claimed—rightly or otherwise—being subjected to an unfair treatment by the state due to the politicized judiciary and law enforcement. In 2004–2012, the UNM controlled all branches of power. This boosted efficiency but shrank time for consensus building. Taken aback by the pace of change and/or nudged by the authorities to do more to contribute to this change, certain businesspeople complained that the state was too ubiquitous. An enhanced state economic activism in the last months before the 2012 elections aimed at an investment-led reduction of Georgia's structural current account deficit, but in the immature institutional context it stirred the business community's doubts. Management of complex expectations and constituencies might have required better stakeholder engagement and smarter multiple move combinations.

   Georgia's 2004–2012 path was akin to a whitewater rafting, with underwater boulders, sharp turns and invisible risks all requiring a rapid reaction. What is the trade-off—where is the inflection point—between efficiency and speed on the one hand and a comprehensive consensus building on the other hand? Beware those with easy answers to this question. They are either dishonest or indifferent.
4. Two weeks before the 2012 parliamentary election, **Georgia was rocked by leaked prison videos**. The first footage—showing a prison guard sodomizing an inmate with a broomstick—was confirmed fake soon after the elections. Its author—a prison guard with alleged record of abusing inmates—went on to co-found a political union promising Russian pensions for all pensioners, double citizenship with Russia and legalization of Russian military bases in Georgia (Russia had ended its military presence in Georgia in 2007) before disappearing from public eye. A second footage showed prison guards beating inmates and it was real.

Fighting crime from 2004, the authorities met resistance, including in the form of prison riots which were forcefully suppressed. Disruption of prison hierarchies which since Georgia's Soviet years had influenced the society was the precondition to other reforms. In 2003–2012, Georgia's prison population increased almost threefold, including due to a heavy-handed prosecution of the economic crime. In Georgia's interconnected society, this was causing discontent.

This provided a fertile ground for the prison videos which were reportedly leaked months after they had been made to maximize the electoral impact. The authorities were caught off guard. Immediate removal of officials handling prisons and resignation of the Minister of Interior did not help. Emotions spilled over and people flocked to streets. Proliferation of broader false narratives—that thousands of Georgian men were being raped in prisons—ensued and took the society by storm. Fact-based analysis and reporting took a pause. Promising to uphold human rights, the GD hit a home run.

5. Another electoral blow came on 30 September 2012, the day before the elections. **A toddler was found drowned** in a wine cellar of her house. Live broadcast from the victim's village—a graphic content thereof—stunned the nation. A number of the GD's leaders speaking live from that village alluded—in the absence of any evidence—to the UNM's responsibility (the toddler's aunt was the GD's local party activist). An investigation launched by the GD after the elections found zero evidence of the UNM's involvement. The toddler's mother soon said that she had no reasons to blame the UNM. But on 1 October 2012 the UNM ended up in a political checkmate.
6. **The GD's economic promise**—that growth would skyrocket, hundreds of new enterprises would be built, unemployment and poverty would soon be defeated, salaries, pensions and subsidies would rise substantially, utility payments and gasoline prices would decrease, debts would be written off, people would benefit from zero interest loans, etc.—came with a strong indiscriminate vilification of Georgia's all achievements in 2004–2012. Mr. Ivanishvili's mythical personality instilled hope in many that he knew a shortcut to prosperity. His statement that "the first year [after the 2012 elections] will be difficult, the second year will be much better, in the third year people will feel progress on their own selves and on their pockets and the fourth year will be excellent" was the promise of

a breakthrough in one electoral term. It swayed voters, including those whose understanding of the state building was shallow or biased and whose memories of Georgia before 2003 were sketchy.

7. **The GD's geopolitical proposition**—that it might be possible to improve relations with Russia *and* advance integration with the West—discounted Russia's zero-sum vision for the region and Georgia's painful post-Soviet experience. Mr. Ivanishvili de facto promised to resolve the dichotomy between being part of the West and maintaining normal relations with Russia. Some voters gave him the benefit of the doubt.
8. **The GD's democratic promise**—that the GD "would build a democracy which would amaze even the West"—stroke a chord with parts of the society which wanted to end UNM's political monopoly, to reinforce checks and balances and to improve the administration of justice.

   In 2004–2012, strengthened and modernized public institutions were insufficiently matched by a restraining infrastructure of an independent administration of justice. The situation was meant to change toward the second half of the period explained in this book, although multiple hybrid risks from Russia and the war of 2008 created a sense of insecurity which resulted in the consolidation of power by the Georgian authorities, including through vigilance by the politicized law enforcement agencies. The government might have become too ubiquitous and too omnipotent. Georgia thus missed the inflection point which, in more benign geopolitical circumstances, would have marked a shift toward better checks and balances. The GD capitalized on the situation.

Leaders act on opportunities; procrastinators are taken aback by threats. Georgia of 2004–2012 acted on opportunities. According to the world chess champion Garry Kasparov, "...when your pawns advance, you gain space to maneuver your pieces, but at the expense of weakening your defences."[1] What generates a larger discontent—a bold action which jolts a society out of its comfort zone for the sake of building a positive legacy or a strategic procrastination which prevents discontent from spilling over but perpetuates mediocre outcomes?

[1] G. Kasparov (2008).

CHAPTER 20

The Margin of Error

Abstract This chapter discusses Georgia's economic convergence with high-income countries and political, geopolitical, cultural, educational, institutional and governance-related preconditions for Georgia's sustained development.

Keywords Convergence · State building · Politics · Demographics · Security · Leadership · Legacy

History is scarce on examples of third-world-to-first-world transitions. "The Singapore story" is the exception and not the rule. Many countries are in low- and middle-income traps. Economic convergence is difficult even within the European Union (EU), despite the EU serving as the anchor of national security and wealth redistribution.

In 2004–2012, Georgia's GDP per capita more than quadrupled from approximately US$ 1,000 to US$ 4,400—a significant achievement under challenging conditions. According to the World Bank, Georgia shifted from a low-income to an upper middle-income group. Still, in 2012, Georgia was poorer than most of the countries in Europe (Fig. 20.1). Georgia's export of goods and services on a per capita basis in 2012—US$

D. Gvindadze, *The Transformation of Georgia from 2004 to 2012*,
https://doi.org/10.1007/978-3-031-18264-8_20

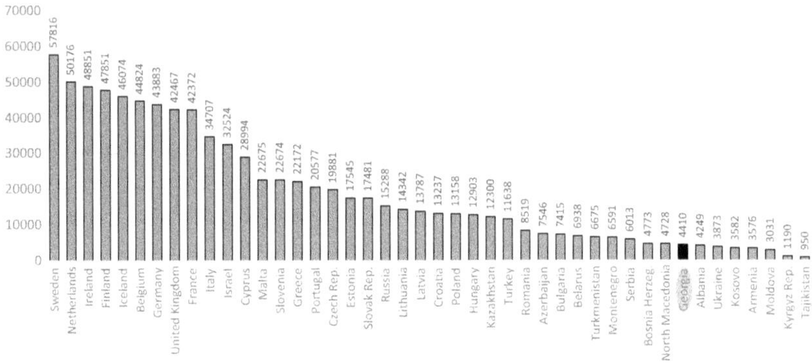

Fig. 20.1 GDP per capita, current prices, US$, 2012 (*Source* International Monetary Fund. World Economic Outlook Database [October 2020])

1600—was nine times lower than in the EU.[1] Georgia trailed the EU on the International Monetary Fund's export diversification and export quality indexes.[2] In 2004–2012, it ran current account deficits which due to the disruption of the Soviet-era trade and manufacturing infrastructure were mainly structural. External rebalancing of the economy in the context of a high growth was, therefore, a priority.

In 2012, I imagined Georgia's economic convergence with high-income countries in the context of five scenarios in Fig. 20.2. My choice of the 2021 forecasting horizon in the Fig. 20.2 was deliberate. It spanned nine years or two electoral terms, similar to the 2004–2012 period explained in this book. In the 3, 5, 7 and 10% *real* growth[3] scenarios, I assumed a GDP deflator (annual price increase) of 5% and a constant US$/GEL exchange rate. The last scenario—18% annual *nominal* growth of GDP per capita in US$ terms—assumed the same

[1] World Bank, World Development Indicators Database (retrieved in March 2021).

[2] IMF Macroeconomic and Financial Data; Export Diversification and Quality, https://data.imf.org/?sk=A093DF7D-E0B8-4913-80E0-A07CF90B44DB (retrieved in March 2021).

[3] Real growth means growth in *volume* of production, which does not include the price (*value*) effect.

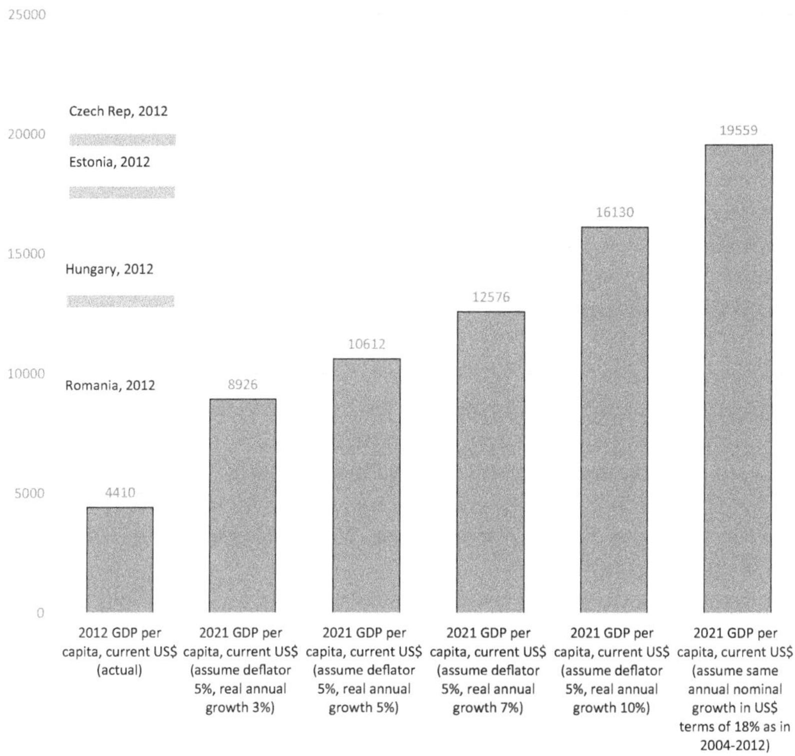

Note: Nominal US$-denominated GDP per capita does not allow to compare *purchasing power* of individuals across countries: same items cost less in Georgia than in France; hence, same US$ income buys more in Georgia that in France. This can be addressed by comparing GDPs per capita in purchasing power parity terms. Still, in this figure, I use GDP per capita in current US$ because this is a good proxy for Georgia's convergence with high-income countries in the EU

Source: International Monetary Fund. World Economic Outlook Database (October 2020); own calculations)

Fig. 20.2 Georgia's economic convergence scenarios

annual *nominal* growth as in 2004–2012.[4] Figure 20.2 also shows 2012 GDP per capita in Romania, Hungary, Estonia and the Czech Republic.

These scenarios were meant to be subject to a considerable degree of uncertainty. As countries progress to higher levels of GDP per capita, high

[4] 18% was a compound annual growth rate of Georgia's US$ denominated GDP per capita in 2004–2012.

growth rates become more difficult to maintain. Populations of several Central and Eastern European countries have stagnated or shrank in the last two decades as people moved westward on their quest for opportunities (Georgia's population shrank by 10% since 2000). Geopolitics and domestic politics and their impact on inflation, growth and exchange rates cannot be predicted in the long run. For example, in 2014–2016, all national currencies in the region came under pressure (explained in Chapter 12) and the COVID-19 crisis from 2020 particularly hit countries like Georgia which export hospitality services.

Georgia's convergence with high-income countries can only materialize if:

- Georgia succeeds in its pursuit of the European and Euroatlantic integration. In the current geopolitical context, this entails complex and risky battles which test the resolve of Georgia's leaders, strength of the national security infrastructure, maturity of citizens, wisdom, foresight and audacity of the West. Much depends on the course of Russia's geopolitical revisionism.
- National security and law enforcement is the unconditional national priority underpinned by a resilient multistakeholder consensus. A country—unless protected by a strong national security infrastructure which predicts and acts upon threats—is built on quicksand, irrespective of quality of economic policies.
- Politicians compete without trespassing red lines, without hollowing out each others'—and their supporters'—living space after elections, and without compromising on a reasonable political neutrality and integrity of key public institutions.
- Economic decisions are technically sound and reasonably ring-fenced from electoral cycles; politics respects private property rights and is geared toward promotion of economic freedom and toward alignment of social entitlements with economic fundamentals.
- National leaders forge resilient social contracts and maintain a socially and culturally acceptable balance between preservation of such economic freedom and facilitation of rapid growth through a resolute state building.
- Education equips with technical skills for the modern marketplace, with critical thinking skills which serve as the first line of defense against populism and hybrid threats, and with empathy, emotional intelligence and right values for a proper exercise of civic duties.

- Leaders consolidate the nation, lead and inspire, reach out beyond party lines, keep faith with the people, imbue hope, fight ideological apathy, stay beyond reproach and implement bold projects—"reference transactions"—which attract big investors.

The laws of aerodynamics are unforgiving. Fly too slow and an aircraft loses lift, stalls and dives. Fly too fast and an aircraft disintegrates due to supersonic shockwaves and pressures. The safe interval between stalling and disintegrating is short, which imposes ruthless margins of error on pilots and flight management systems.

A state building in developing countries at geopolitical fault lines happens at lower altitudes, though margins of error are equally ruthless. Successful legacies can only be created by visionary, courageous and altruist state builders through multiple electoral cycles. The ultimate legacy of Georgia's state building explained in this book depends on the outcome of the new global battle between democracy and autocracy.

Bibliography

D. Gvindadze (2017), "The Transformation of Georgia from 2004 to 2012: State Building, Reforms, Growth and Investments", *Palgrave Macmillan*.

Presentations made at various times in 2004–2012 by the Ministry of Finance of Georgia, National Bank of Georgia and the Government of Georgia. Georgian Reform—Success Stories (December 2009). *Presentation by the Government of Georgia* (2009).

Geostat's (Georgian statistical agency) databases.

D. Gvindadze (2012), "Walking the Walk in Public Budgeting", *Financial Times*, July 19, 2012.

L. Gurgenidze (2009), "Georgia's Search for Economic Liberty: A Blueprint for Reform in Developing Economies", *American Enterprise Institute for Policy Research*, no. 2.

World Bank (2012), "Fighting Corruption in Public Services: Chronicling Georgia's Reforms".

M. Porter (2008), "On Competition", *Harvard Business Press*.

Ernst & Young and Ministry of Finance of Georgia (2012), Georgia Pocket Tax Book.

World Bank (2009), "Reshaping Economic Geography", *World Development Report*.

McKinsey Global Institute—Research on Urbanization (http://www.mckinsey.com/insights).

N. Beruashvili, O. McGill (2010), "Breaking Up the Logjam: Automated Customs Risk Management System Implementation in Georgia", *International Finance Corporation, Smartlessons*.

Chemonics International Inc. (2009), "Georgia: Open For Business", *Georgia Business Climate Reform Final Report*.

D. Gvindadze, *The Transformation of Georgia from 2004 to 2012*,
https://doi.org/10.1007/978-3-031-18264-8

Georgia Rising: Sustaining Rapid Economic Growth (2013), *World Bank, Country Economic Memorandum.*

Georgia Public Service Hall home page.

World Bank (2013), Doing Business 2013: Smarter Regulations for Small and Medium-Size Enterprises. Washington, DC: World Bank Group. DOI: https://doi.org/10.1596/978-0-8213-9615-5. License: Creative Commons Attribution CC BY 3.0.

L. K. Yew (2000), "From Third World to First. The Singapore Story: 1965–2000", *HarperCollins Publishers.*

P. Pomerantsev, G. Robertson, J. Ratkovic and A. Applebaum (2014), "Revolutionary Tactics: Insights from Police and Justice Reform in Georgia", *Legatum Institute Transition Forum.*

C. Reinhart and K. Rogoff (2009), "This Time is Different: Eight Centuries of Financial Folly", *Prinston University Press.*

N. Taleb (2010), "The Black Swan. The Impact of the Highly Improbable", *Penguin Books.*

D. Acemoglu and J. A. Robinson (2013), Why Nations Fail: The Origins of Power, Prosperity, and Poverty, *Crown Business New York.*

Georgia's Hydropower Potential, Giving Water the Green Light (June 28, 2012), Bank of Georgia Research.

Public Opinion Survey, Residents of Georgia (September–October 2019), Center for Insights in Survey Research, a Project of the International Republican Institute.

P. Zelikow, E. Edelman, K. Harrison, C. Ward Gventer (July/August 2020), The Rise of Strategic Corruption, How States Weaponise Graft. *Foreign Affairs.*

M. Galeotti (2018), The Vory—Russia's Super Mafia, *Yale University Press.*

Georgian National Study (June–July 2012), International Republican Institute.

The World Prison Brief database https://www.prisonstudies.org/

World Development Report "Reshaping Economic Geography" (2009), *World Bank*

Georgian Economy—Need for a New Economic Model in the Context of Global Change (June 2020). *Galt & Taggart.*

Bendukidze, Roeder, Tanner, Urushadze (2014), Healthcare Reform in the Republic of Georgia, a Healthcare Reform Roadmap for Post-Semashko Countries and Beyond. ISBN: 1497422000; ISBN-13: 978-1497422001.

N. Gilauri (2017), Practical Economics, *Palgrave Pivot.*

The Georgian Hospital Sector, Transparency International Georgia (Tbilisi, 2012).

The Georgian Health insurance Industry, Transparency International Georgia (Tbilisi, 2012).

The World Bank Pension Reform Primer 45728, "The World Bank Pension Conceptual Framework".

Ministry of Finance of Georgia, Statistical Bulletin of Public Debt of Georgia N1, December 2013.

Reimagining Tax Authorities for the Future (16 October 2020), *McKinsey & Company.*

The Global Laundromat: How Did it Work and Who Benefited? (20 March 2017), *The Guardian.*

Georgia: Financial System Stability Assessment (November 2001), IMF Country Report No. 01/210.

National Development Banks are Back in Vogue (March 7, 2019), *The Economist.*

World Development Report "Reshaping Economic Geography" (2009), *The World Bank.*

Tourism in Georgia, Monthly Market Watch (May 2019), *Galt & Taggart.*

United Nations Data Booklet "The World's Cities in 2018".

E. Luce (2017), The Retreat of Western Liberalism. *Little, Brown.*

Caves, Frankel, Jones. World Trade and Payments, an Introduction, Ninth Edition (2002). *Addison Wesley.*

Z. Gáková and L. Dijkstra. European Union Regional Policy no. 02/2008, Labour Mobility Between the Regions of the EU-27 and a Comparison with the USA.

Is the Franco-German Plan Europe's 'Hamiltonian' Moment? EU Coronavirus Recovery Fund Proposal Puts Fiscal Union Back on the Agenda. (May 21, 2020) *Financial Times.*

Singapore IMF country report No. 18/245, July 2018.

G. Kasparov (2008), How Life Imitates Chess: Insights into Life as a Game of Strategy, *Bloomsbury.*

Index

D. Gvindadze, *The Transformation of Georgia from 2004 to 2012*,
https://doi.org/10.1007/978-3-031-18264-8

www.ingramcontent.com/pod-product-compliance
Ingram Content Group UK Ltd.
Pitfield, Milton Keynes, MK11 3LW, UK
UKHW020836290926
15470UKWH00004B/1372
* 9 7 8 3 0 3 1 1 8 2 6 3 1 *